BOARD

SURF/SKATE/SNOW GRAPHICS

LAURENCE KING  CREATIVE REVIEW

A Creative Review Book
First published in Great Britain in 1997
Second edition published 2003 by Laurence King Publishing Ltd
71 Great Russell Street
London WC1B 3BP
United Kingdom
Tel: +44 20 7430 8850
Fax: +44 20 7430 8880
e-mail: enquiries@laurenceking.co.uk
www.laurenceking.co.uk

A catalogue record for this book is available from the British Library.

ISBN 1 85669 327 9

Written by Patrick Burgoyne
Designed by Jeremy Leslie

Consultant Editor Lewis Blackwell

Printed in Hong Kong

INTRO

INTRO

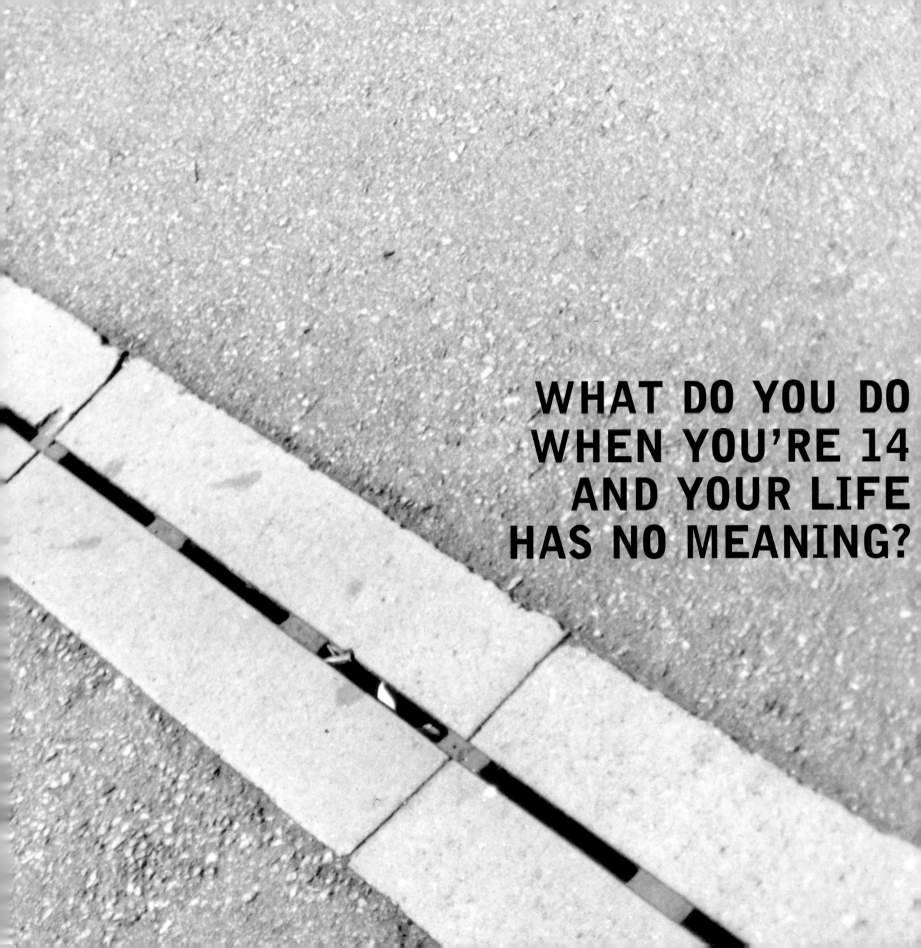

WHAT DO YOU DO
WHEN YOU'RE 14
AND YOUR LIFE
HAS NO MEANING?

THRILLS CAN BE PRETTY
THIN ON THE GROUND
IN LATE TWENTIETH
CENTURY SUBURBIA.

Since the 1960s, capitalism's disaffected, disinclined youth have increasingly turned to board sports in an attempt to find a reason for getting out of bed. By creating their own verbal and visual languages, codes of behaviour, dress and ethics, the inextricably linked, yet subtly different cultures of surfing, skateboarding and snowboarding give focus to lives rendered desperate by the hormonally-induced chaos that is puberty.

All three have created complex and sophisticated subcultures which have proved enduringly influential in the worlds of fashion, design and music. Be it surf, skate or snow, board sports share aspects of a common culture and a common propensity for spawning some of the strongest contemporary graphic expression. Unusually, there exists a strong link between those who do and those who make: the vast majority of the graphic artists who decorate the boards are riders themselves.

These graphics are vital: "People buy boards because of the way they look. Eighty to 90 per cent buy them for looks only, not how they perform," says Matt Micuda who has been designing graphics on surfboards for 15 years. "An entire line can be a flop if you don't get the graphics right." No other sports or youth cultures give such a central role to graphic design.

John Hersey is one of America's leading illustrators. He believes that board sports are producing the most interesting graphics in the USA today. "The graphics came from the street originally," he says. "That is, they have come from the surfers,

"WE'RE ONE BIG TARGET MARKET"

From Flakezine snowboarding website

skaters and snowboarders themselves, much like rave graphics and the 60s concert posters and 'freak' comic art came from the actual people involved in those youth culture movements. I think that the original influence were gas station uniforms and other industrial uniforms that kids could buy real cheap at thrift stores with their elliptical embroidered name patches such as 'Bob' or 'Ed'. These ready-made graphics, plus the influence of the trendy inebriants that the kids were taking, created the roots of the whole look."

An image of rebellion, of offering an alternative lifestyle, has been central to the growth of all three sports but it exists in differing degrees. "Snowboarding is primarily a rich kids' sport," claims Moish Brenman, art director of skateboard company Consolidated Incorporated. "You need $600 for a decent board, you need boots and bindings, then you've got to get to the mountain, get a lift pass. It's not something that any kid can just go out and have fun with. Also it's incredibly easy compared to skateboarding. You see like a 50 year-old guy and his 10 and 12 year old daughters and within an hour they can stand up and within a very short time they can do jumps, and they try to pass it off as this really hard, extreme sport. Snowboarding steals its styles, its tricks, everything. Snowboarding is where skateboarding was three years ago. If you look at the styles, the baggy clothes, the tricks being done it all came from skating. Skateboarders have very little respect for snowboarders.

"Surfing's a bit different, there's almost an ego battle going on as to which is harder but there's a respect for them because surfing's a very difficult sport," he continues "There's an uneasy truce between the two. There's slight animosity because they're jockeying for who's top dog, which is the toughest sport. In so far as graphics are concerned, surfing and skateboarding are not really tied together at all. There are two types of surfer: the hippy cruiser who smokes a lot of pot and wants to be at one with the ocean, then there's the hardcore guy with a shaved head and tribal tattoos. Neither of them is really relevant to skateboarding anymore."

Although the whole aesthetic began with surfing, and surfing styles still exert an influence on snowboards especially, the three sports have split to establish separate, if linked, graphic identities. "Surfing and skateboarding were originally connected because they were done by the same people, but then skateboarding broke away and took its own path," explains Bill Stewart, regarded by many as the leading surfboard graphic artist. "When we go to the trade shows now, we call the skate area 'the dark side' because the surfing side of the hall always seems so much happier and so much more upbeat."

Artist and illustrator Jim Phillips has been involved with surfing, and later skateboarding, since the early 1960s: "Skateboarders are rad. When a surfer falls off he goes 'splash' and it's like 'big deal'. When a skateboarder falls it's on asphalt and it can be life-threatening. It's a gnarly sport and the art has to reflect that.

"With surfing it's mostly drinking and parties and the surf bum lifestyle where you don't work, it's more passive," Phillips continues. "Skaters are more aggressive. They have to fight to find places to skate, when they go out skating it's almost like they're going to war."

"When I was a kid [in Santa Cruz] I used to get beat up for skateboarding by rednecks and guys in big trucks," says Brenman. "We got kicked out of every place we went, chased by the cops, chased by business owners. We were outcasts and I think that perception is what then fed into a lot of the graphics."

Similarly, snowboarders encountered a great deal of hostility from skiers when they first started to compete for space on crowded slopes. Although outright confrontation has died away now, the relish for rule-breaking remains.

As well as different attitudes, the sports have different target markets. "Generally, surfers are more conservative," says Matt Micuda. "A lot of surfers are like 40 year-old doctors earning good money and they won't worry about spending $500, $600 on a surfboard. The clientele has a lot more money and the graphics have to be geared toward them."

Jim Phillips agrees: "The graphics weren't wild on surfboards for years. You'd just have the company's logo and maybe a few swirls done in resin or colour on the rails. A surfboard is a personal thing, it's almost like something you wear so you don't want some big ugly thing on it."

Similarly, with snowboards, the investment is far greater than for skateboards and the object is meant to last a lot longer. "There are big differences in doing graphics for skateboards and snowboards," says Brian Krezel, art director at Maple skateboards. "Right from the planning stage you've got to think differently. You have to remember that a snowboard may be on the

"SKATE DREAMS:
1-IMMORTALITY
2-TO SKATE EVERY
PARK IN THE WORLD
3-TO HIT PAUSE ON
A COOL FEELING
4-TO DIE ON
YOUR BOARD"

From Thrasher skateboarding magazine, January 1997

shelves for nine months and it may be in someone's possession for years. With a skateboard, the most important thing is to get it off the shelf and into the kid's hands as quick as possible. Skateboard graphics are almost disposable, the graphic will be gone in a couple of weeks anyway. As soon as someone starts to use the board the graphics get scratched off and kids cover them over with stickers. Snowboards have to be more aesthetic and pleasing or people will get sick of them in a year."

Skateboards, which retail in the USA for around $60 to $70 and in the UK for the pound equivalent, come out in new designs every month, whereas snowboards usually appear in a line of new designs each autumn. Surfboards, on the other hand, are often one-offs specially painted to the specifications of the customer. They are highly personalized objects.

Most surfboard companies are small operations run by pros or ex-pros. Designer David Carson had a line of surfboards when he was a pro, before continuing his association with board sports by designing surfing, skateboarding and snowboarding magazines. The larger companies will have a stable of sponsored team riders and produce boards bearing their names – which is also the norm for skateboard and snowboard companies. Thus board sports offer kids as young as 14 the chance to fulfil what for many of them is a dream – to go professional and, thus, to drop out of school.

These pros establish a reputation by taking part in competitions and appearing in magazines and videos. The most popular ones become merchandizing phenomena and will sell hundreds of boards simply because the boards bear their names.

Pros will sit down with their company's designer and discuss the graphics for their endorsed boards, often bringing in ideas torn from favourite comics or magazines; sometimes they will ask for the logo of a favourite brand or the face of a favourite film star to be applied to their board. Some riders expect the in-house artist to interpret their ideas, while others bring in rough sketches, but many more are artists themselves. The likes of Mark Gonzales and Neil Blender in skateboarding and Jamie Lynn in snowboarding have become almost as admired for their art as their riding.

Most board designers, whether in-house or not, take part in the sport themselves, although opinion is divided as to whether this is vital. "Usually the artists are boarders themselves – I'd say in 80 per cent of cases," says Jeff Bartel, art director at

Morrow snowboards. "I don't think that it is necessary but it definitely helps." Design consultancy Jager DiPaola Kemp, based in Burlington, Vermont creates all the graphics for Burton, the snowboard market leader. Design director David Covell says: "Our whole team snowboards, it's really important. It's also how we do most of our research. When you get out there you can talk to a lot of riders and find out what they really want." Even freelancers need some understanding of the sports that they want to design for. "The number one thing I look for before I've even opened their portfolio is who are they? Do they skate or snowboard? Are they for real? If you don't the stuff isn't going to translate – it just comes out wrong," explains John Thomas, art director at World Industries which makes both skate- and snowboards. "I need to see that they have some knowledge of the market or the right kind of oddball mentality. You could be 35 and still have the mentality. God knows, I'm going to be 30 next year."

But taking part in these dangerous sports can be a little hazardous to the unwary designer. "I almost broke my drawing finger skateboarding," says Jim Phillips. "The team riders didn't think I was really a skater because I didn't do it anymore but I just couldn't take the risk – I'm like Betty Grable with her billion dollar legs."

Having experience of the sports also helps in coping with the problems of designing for such peculiarly-shaped objects, although, again, opinion is divided as to whether it is always best to design with the shape of the board in mind, even within the same sport. "You're working with something that's eight inches wide and 32 inches long with curved ends and you have to design for that shape," claims skateboard designer Brenman. "A lot of people don't seem to think like that – they just take some graphic and try to make it fit – but that doesn't work." But Erik Brunetti of rival skateboard company Fuct takes a diametrically opposed view: "I never design to the board shape. I always do it any size that works then I put the design into the computer and shrink it down. I think designing to the shape is too predictable. I like it when images or words get cropped off."

Fuct, as the name suggests, is a company that has taken the rebelliousness that characterizes all three board sports to new heights... or should that be depths? When forming the company six years ago, Brunetti deliberately set out to exploit a gap in the market by using controversial, often sexually explicit graphics on Fuct's boards and clothing. Though an extreme case, his experience sums up a lot of what people find attractive about board sports. "I did it because kids want to piss off their parents," he says. "They want to feel part of some elite group. When they buy Fuct they think they're buying more than product – they're buying an attitude. Fuct presents a certain way of life in the same way that punk rock did in the 1970s."

That way of life is what has attracted the attention of an advertising world keen to lend street credibility to big brands. But they only want to take on the aesthetic on their own terms. "People try to capture the attitude but there's no way companies are going to be able to sell the aesthetic to millions of people in its raw form," says Scott Clum, art director of Ray Gun Publishing's snowboarding magazine, Stick, and former art director at Morrow snowboards. "Initially what attracts them is an attitude ten storeys high, but once Nike or Coke is done with it, it's two inches tall."

Board sports pride themselves on their "alternative" or underground credentials, the need to "keep it real", so that any company seeking to appropriate their aesthetic for blatant commercial gain will attract the ire of the hardcore. Surfers, skateboarders and snowboarders have created not just sports but bodies of values concerning politics, fashion, art and music which find expression through graphics and through which they have established their own place within popular culture.

"Their graphics help these kids to define themselves as a unique tribal entity," says John Hersey. "Through their graphics, they have set themselves apart from the rest of society. It is an aesthetic of rebellion and that's what makes it so fascinating and so inspiring to me."

In the face of encroaching commercialism they frequently subvert the vernacular. Popular cartoon characters have been given that certain twist which has come to be seen, rightly or wrongly, as embodying the genre. Skateboard company World Industries, and artist Marc McKee in particular, lead the way with Disney as a prime target. Winnie the Pooh was pictured with a jar of money instead of honey, while Beauty and the Beast had wild sex.

McKee's 1992 skateboard entitled Accidental Gun Death shows how other graphic genres have also been subverted. Hand drawn in comic-book style, it depicts the moment when two parents discover that their son has just killed his brother with their own gun. The graphic style suggests

something aimed at children but the content is dark – as dark as anything produced by the underground comics scene. Is this supposed to be funny or a powerful condemnation of America's gun laws? And what is it doing on what, after all, is a toy?

Music has exerted a constant influence, most recently with hip-hop but, earlier, with punk which found a natural ally in surfing and skateboarding. While its challenge to the establishment manifested itself in Britain in bondage trousers, Mohawk haircuts and Jamie Reid's ransom note graphics, punk in the USA was embraced by surfers and skateboarders. It had a huge influence on graphics in both sports, setting designers free to experiment as never before. Similarly, the influence of rave culture, coupled with the desire to resist corporate America, led to a plethora of ripped-off logos appearing on skateboards and snowboards especially. Whole companies dealt in nothing else.

"This area has been the place where music culture becomes visible," says Aaron Betsky, curator of architecture and design at the Museum of Modern Art in San Francisco. The art world has become increasingly interested in board sports. Aaron Rose, of the Alleged Gallery in New York, runs a touring exhibition of skateboard art, while Bill Stewart reports having painted at least 150 surfboards for clients to hang on their walls as art objects. Betsky chose a snowboard and a surfboard for his museum's exhibition of icons of American culture. He believes the value of the board sports aesthetic is as "a vehicle through which the world of the street becomes honed down by its audience and translated into a selling tool by a wider graphic community. It has acted as a funnel for what is going on in street culture so that it feeds back into the commercial world of design and advertising."

Through the pages of this book it is possible to trace the myriad influences on youth culture over the last 30 years. There are psychedelic or hippy influences. Adolescent satanic gore fests betray the hand of heavy metal. The underground comics scene is well represented, as are racing stripes and the cheesy glamour of the 1970s hot-rod scene. Manga takes a bow, as does Japanese kitsch. Favoured film stars or cartoon characters come and go. Grunge and techno, hip-hop and punk – all are there but only after passing through the filter of the differing sensibilities of surfing, skateboarding and snowboarding. Trends change but the attitude remains.

"A VISUAL INSULT TO THE LATE TWENTIETH CENTURY"

Mambo surfwear slogan

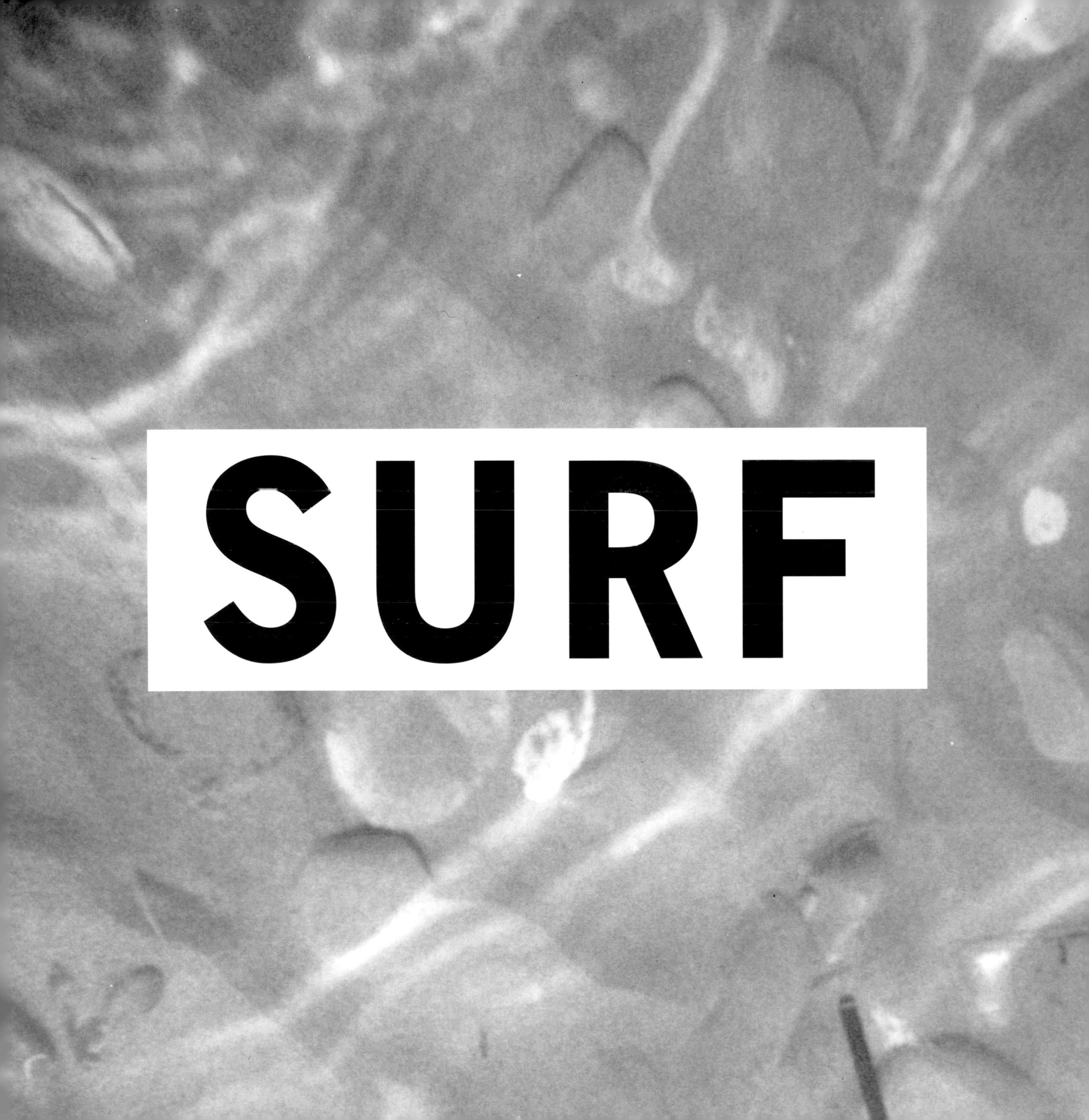

SURF

ЯЯUS

It is commonly assumed that the first surfers were Hawaiian fishermen in canoes who used to ride in to shore on the waves. The first Western visitors to the islands in the eighteenth century described local people standing on wooden boards and riding waves. By then, as Nat Young describes in The History of Surfing (1983, Palm Beach Press), surfing had become part of Hawaiian religion and culture with strict rules governing which class of the population was allowed to use which boards and which beaches.

Young recounts how the arrival of Christian missionaries in the nineteenth century, and with it the imposition of Victorian moral repression, led to the suppression of surfing in Hawaii. It was not until the beginning of the twentieth century that young Hawaiians returned to surfing as purely a leisure pursuit and introduced it to, first, the USA in 1907 and then Australia in 1915. These early surfers rode solid redwood boards weighing over 150 pounds a time. The introduction of balsa wood in the 1930s and then fibreglass in the 1940s changed the sport dramatically, making boards lighter, easier to handle and allowing surfers to perform many new tricks.

Up until the 1950s, decoration on surfboards had been pretty much restricted to manufacturers' logos or the patterns created by combining alternate strips of dark (redwood) and light (balsa) wood in the boards' construction. These patterns, where the darker wood was used along the rails, or edges, of the board to add strength, are still

reflected in boards today: the rails are often picked out in bright colours and stripes are still a common theme.

In the 1950s surfing's popularity increased enormously, especially in California. The beginnings of today's surf culture were portrayed in countless B-movies and in a rash of surfing magazines. Surf music, by artists such as Dick Dale and later The Beach Boys, was invented and surfing slang entered the language. Surfers came to be seen as wild young things, holding raucous beach parties and frequently running into trouble with landlords who tried to stop them trekking over their land in order to gain access to the ocean.

Graphically, the hot-rodding scene had a big influence, with surfers adopting racing stripes and competition numbers on their boards. These early decorations were applied by hand using coloured resins which were then "glossed" over to supply the shiny finish which, until recently, was a feature on all boards. In fact the basics of surfboard manufacture have changed relatively little since the 1960s. First a mass-produced polyurethane foam "blank" is roughly shaped and sanded. Then it is usually painted white to stop the sea water turning the foam brown. Next comes "glassing" whereby sheets of fibreglass, for strength, are stuck on to the blank using resin which also makes the board waterproof. Then the board is sanded once again before glossing.

Artist Jim Phillips started in the surfboard manufacturing business as a glasser in 1962. When colleagues discovered he could draw he was switched to decorating the boards, which delighted Phillips as he was keen to escape the toxic fumes that were a common hazard in surfboard manufacture. At Florida's Oceanside surfboards in 1968 he became one of the first artists to experiment with an airbrush. His designs did not sell well and he abandoned the technique (ten years later airbrushing became the most popular means of applying graphics the world over). In 1971, at Overlin, Phillips made further innovations developing a "scratchboard" style whereby graphics were applied using pen and Indian ink and then worked into the board using a trim knife to add texture and shading. Then, the deck would be glossed and the result resembled scrimshaw, the technique by which sailors used to engrave shells. His designs were a significant step forward, featuring full illustrations of subjects such as horseback riders and eagles. Phillips believes he must have produced hundreds of surfboards in this way, taking around two hours to create each one.

During the late 1960s and early 1970s, Phillips became a leading figure in the explosion in surfboard graphics that accompanied the hippy era. "The whole thing hadn't really been established yet, we just did whatever popped into our heads," he says. "It was the psychedelic era so there were lots of references to that and we started doing Pop Art things because Andy Warhol was a big influence. In the early 1970s I did a lot of Beatles portraits. They threw everything at me – I was even asked to do the rise and fall of the Roman Empire on a surfboard."

By putting familiar figures from the popular culture of the day, including Superman and Donald Duck, on a surfboard, and doing it without the copyright holders' permission, Phillips' work was a precursor to much of what followed in skateboarding graphics. Indeed, it was no accident that he later became a highly influential figure in skateboarding through his work as the art director for Santa Cruz, one of the first major skateboarding companies.

In the late 1970s, the combination of two elements created the next step forward in surfboard graphics – the airbrush and punk. Airbrushing, where paint is sprayed under pressure on to the surface of the board, allows for very speedy working. This is very important with surfboard manufacture because the margins are notoriously tight and labour costs at a premium. Even today, artists can be paid as little as $30 for a spray job with $10 being enough to have the rails of your board painted in the colours of your

choice. By using airbrushes, artists could quickly create far more intricate works, and in far less time, than they could using coloured resins.

This was just as well because the explosion of punk led to demands from customers for ever more adventurous designs. "Punk broke down the barriers so that there were no rules in surfboard art," says Bill Stewart of Stewart Surfboards in San Clemente, California, who Jim Phillips cites as the best surfboard artist around. Because, even today, each surfboard is hand-made and hand-decorated individually, there is a high degree of personalization in the graphics. Some companies do produce lines of boards with a particular graphic, and artists like Stewart may have a book of standard designs that they can do, but as often as not customers request their own graphics. Punk's popularity among surfers led to its aesthetic being extended to surfboard decoration. "Before, there was nothing controversial about the graphics at all. In the punk era I had all sorts of crazy requests," Stewart recalls. "One guy wanted a picture of a poodle being run over by a car. I asked him why and he said 'because my mom's got one'."

A Californian band by the name of Surf Punks became briefly popular.

"They had skateboard wheels on their guitars and a song that went 'my beach. Fuck off'," says Damion Fuller, a designer at Australian surfwear company Mambo. The band was one of the first to apply newly-available fluorescent inks and paints to the surf scene. "They used to come on stage in fluorescent wetsuits and that launched the whole fluoro thing worldwide," says Fuller. Soon fluoro paints became a common sight on surfboards. Artists broke away from the smooth realism of airbrush portraits and scenes and began experimenting with abstract techniques. Bill Stewart even remembers dipping a tennis ball in paint and bouncing it across a surfboard in search of a new effect.

But surfing was becoming big business and during the 1980s the consequences of big money professionalism began to be felt. Professional riders became anxious that intricate illustrations might detract from the impact and visibility of their sponsors' logos which were printed on the nose of the board. Also, it was discovered that using a rougher finish which attempted to replicate the effects of a shark's skin made boards lighter and faster and so the traditional glossing method was abandoned by pros. Unfortunately, some of the boards' strength came from this gloss as well as the multiple layers of fibreglass which pros were using as few as possible of in order to reduce weight. The new boards broke much more easily — especially when surfers performed the new jumping and spinning tricks which they were beginning to copy from skateboarding. Not many riders thought it worth paying extra to have a board decorated when it was not going to last very long.

The upshot of all this was that pros started using plain white boards with the only graphics being those of their sponsors. And, because of the way marketing works, ordinary surfers soon copied them. "It was a horrible period for surfing, classic youth exploitation," says Dare Jennings, who runs Mambo. "Decoration became a bad thing."

In the early 1990s, in an effort to bring back decoration, Mambo brought out a line of surfboards bearing simple, strong patterns in bright colours over the full surface of the top of the board. "We used simple, dramatic shapes because price is so important," says Jennings. "Once you spend more than ten minutes painting a board the price doubles so all the designs had to be able to be sprayed up in under

20 minutes." Mambo's bold, bright designs, produced in batches of around 50, include representations of a snooker table, a television set with armchair, camouflage patterns and a lawnmower.

The company has been heralded as leading the way in a return to decoration amid a graphic scene that is more varied than ever before. Full-blown airbrushed figures and scenes are still popular, as is the retro appeal of racing stripes and all things Hawaiian. A new addition is the crossover of graffiti styles as well as skateboard graphics which are now repaying the influence that surfing once had on them. "The whole thing's coming full circle," says leading Californian surfboard artist Matt Micuda. "Right now a lot of designs are being brought back from the 1970s. You're seeing a lot of lines and curves that outline the template of the board. All the psychedelic stuff's coming back and some tricks like applying paint with squeegees rather than the airbrush. All sorts of techniques that were kind of lost are coming back.

"Everybody borrows from everybody else," he continues. "I don't like to use the term 'ripping off' because I think that's kind of harsh. You just borrow things, tweak them and add your own thing. If you're tuned in, you can pick and choose and add your own flavours — it's just like cooking."

By including a surfboard in its 1997 exhibition of 12 icons of American culture, the Museum of Modern Art in San Francisco acknowledged the role that surfing has played, not just in the development of skateboarding and snowboarding culture, but in the popular culture of the world. The associations of freedom, fun and youthful rebellion that a surfboard conjure up make it, as the museum's curator Aaron Betsky says, a highly symbolic object. And the surfboard's shape makes it a great canvas for the artist, as a story from Micuda bears out.

"A friend of mine who knew the famous American painter Sam Francis [a contemporary of Jackson Pollock] once showed him a surfboard. It was all white, no colour on it. He said to him 'Next time you get a surfboard made let me paint it — it would make a perfect white canvas and that shape is wonderful'. So he did. My friend rode it a few times and then later on he wanted to take a surf trip but needed some more money. So he sold the painted Sam Francis surfboard to an art dealer in France — for $20,000. It blew my mind!"

Buzzards in the Sky
by Jim Phillips for Overlin, 1971
Scratchboard technique

Donald Duck and Superman
by Jim Phillips for Oceanside, 1968
Airbrush

S&M
by Jimbo Phillips (Jim's son), 1994
Airbrush

Yoda
by Bill Stewart for Stewart Surfboards, 1980
Airbrush

Alaskan motif
by Jim Phillips for Overlin, 1971
Pen, ink and resin

Butterfly Lady
by Bill Stewart, 1981
Airbrush

Dolphins
by Jack Meyer for Local Motion, 1980
Airbrush

Old Man
by Bill Stewart, 1980
Airbrush

**Jimbo Phillips,
1996**
Airbrush

**Bill Stewart,
1980**
Airbrush

**Einstein
by Bill Stewart,
1980**
Airbrush

Jetson family
by Jimbo Phillips,
1994
Airbrush

Previous four pages,
various boards by
**Laura Sue Powers,
1977 to 1997**
Airbrush

**Beavis and
Butthead
by Jimbo Phillips,
1996**
Airbrush

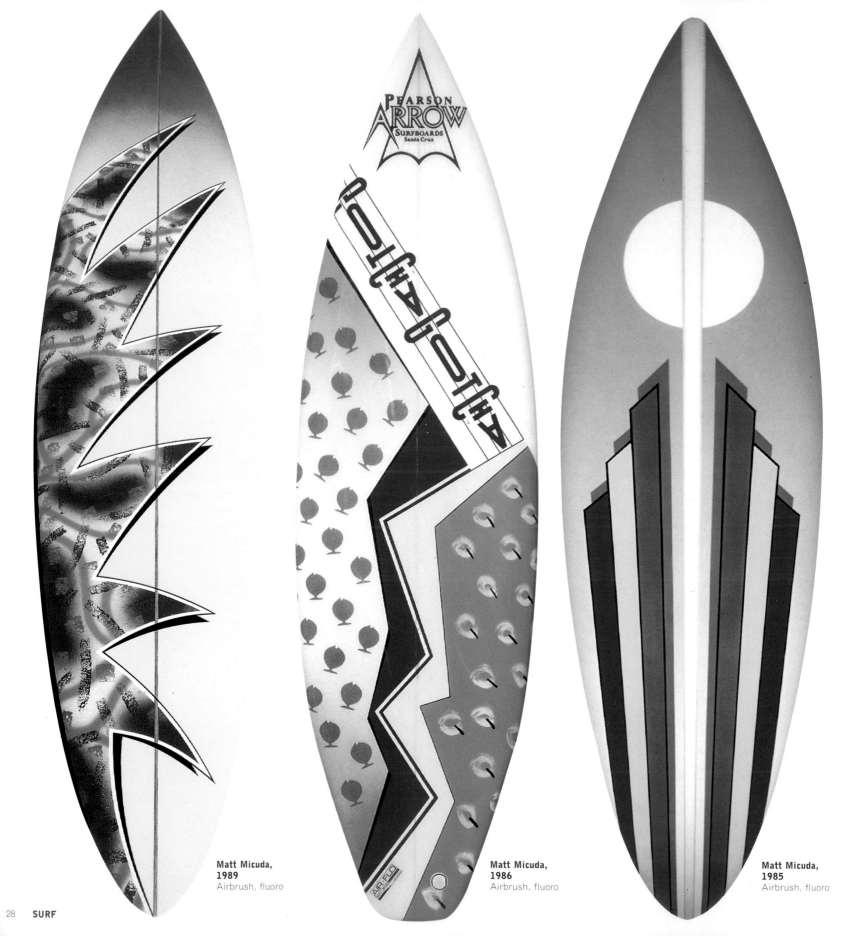

PEARSON
ARROW
SURFBOARDS
Santa Cruz

Matt Micuda,
1989
Airbrush, fluoro

Matt Micuda,
1986
Airbrush, fluoro

Matt Micuda,
1985
Airbrush, fluoro

**Mitch McEwen
for Local Motion, 1995**
Airbrush

**Matt Micuda,
1988**
Airbrush, fluoro

**Matt Micuda,
1988**
Airbrush, fluoro

Ellis "Elvis" Beaton
and Jamie Buckingham
for Gulf Stream,
1997
Airbrush

Sharp Eye,
1997
Airbrush

Ellis "Elvis" Beaton
and Jamie Buckingham
for Gulf Stream, 1997
Airbrush

Sharp Eye,
1997
Airbrush

Mitch McEwen
for Local Motion,
c1995
Airbrush

Sharp Eye,
1997
Airbrush

Ellis "Elvis" Beaton
and Jamie Buckingham
for Gulf Stream, 1997
Airbrush

Mitch McEwen
for Local Motion, 1997
Airbrush

Matt Micuda,
1989
Airbrush, fluoro

Matt Micuda,
1988
Airbrush, fluoro

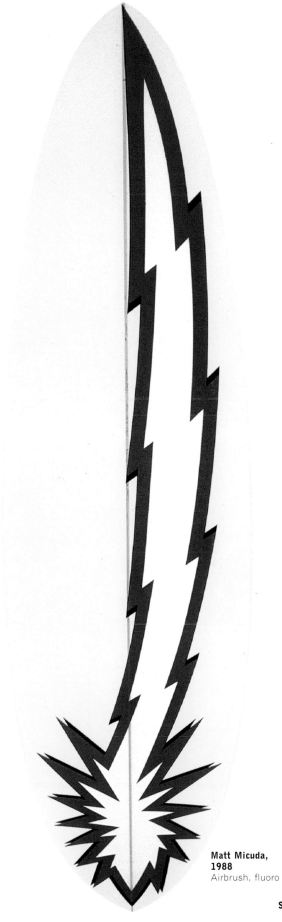

Sharp Eye,
1997
Airbrush

Matt Micuda,
1988
Airbrush, fluoro

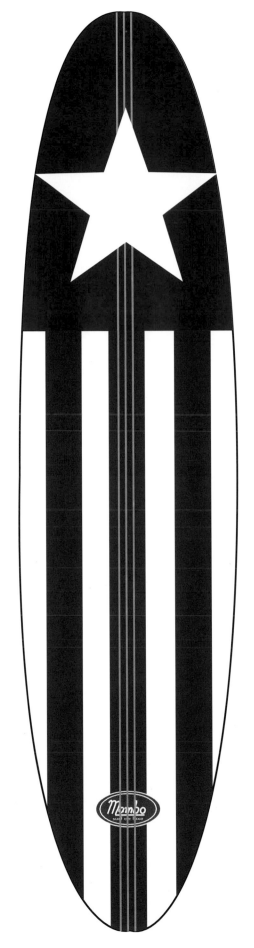

"THE SURFBOARD IS AN ICON OF AMERICAN CULTURE. IT'S A VERY EVOCATIVE OBJECT THAT IS A GREAT STORE OF OUR MEMORIES AND DREAMS."

Aaron Betsky, Curator of Architecture and Design,
Museum of Modern Art, San Francisco

This spread and four
following, all boards
by Paul McNeil
for Mambo, 1996/97
Airbrush

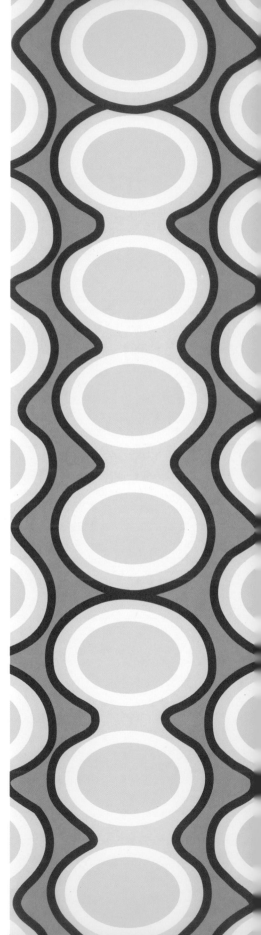

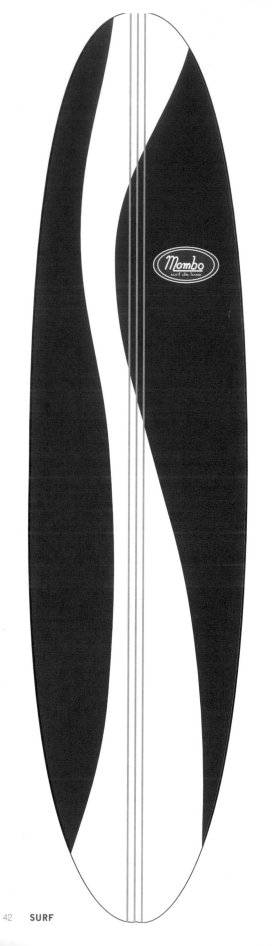

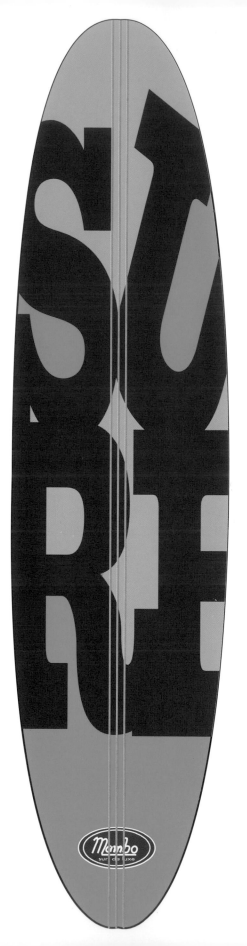

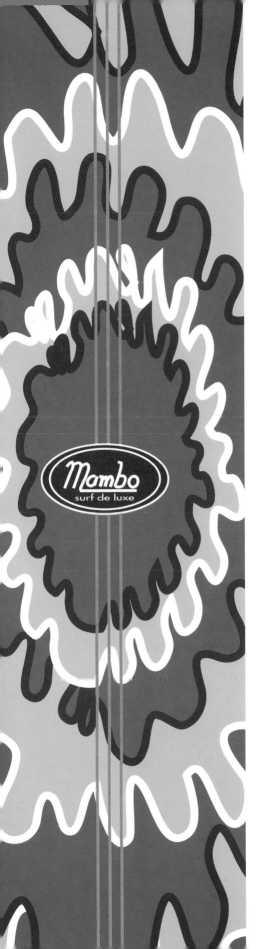

Jim Phillips,
1992
Sticker

SKATE

Depending on who you believe, the first skateboards were made in California in the 1960s, or late 1950s, either from roller-skate wheels attached to a board or from the deck of a child's scooter. It seems most likely that the first skateboarders were surfers looking for something to do when the wave conditions were unfavourable.

The first skateboarding boom came in the early 1970s. Purpose-built skateparks opened up across the USA and, later, Europe, featuring concrete bowls and ramps where skaters could perform their tricks. But skateboarding is a dangerous sport and spiralling insurance costs forced most of the parks to close, sending skaters back on to the streets and public spaces. At this time skateboards did not carry elaborate graphics.

Jim Phillips was art director at Santa Cruz skateboards from 1974 to 1990. "I started doing skateboards with a surfing buddy of mine, Jay Shuirman, who set up Santa Cruz. Back then boards just had a logo on," he explains. "For years I tried to get graphics going. I was doing rock and roll posters at the time and I wanted to do that on boards but it wasn't seen as acceptable until other companies started doing it around 1984. Powell was the first, then later Dogtown, but I hope that we had a lot to do with the development of graphics too."

As Moish Brenman explained in the introduction to this book, once skaters were forced back on to the streets they were hounded by irate citizens because of the destruction that skateboarding causes to handrails and kerbsides as skaters slide, or "grind", along them – and also because of the general "nuisance" caused. This fostered the rebelliousness, fierce independence and rejection of anything seen as corporate or "corp" that developed into the skate attitude. "The serious graphics started in the early 1980s when it was a more underground thing," says Brian Krezel, art director at Maple. "The big fat boards came in – around ten inches wide – and you had this big wide space of wood and companies thought 'hey, why not silk screen it'. They're the earliest graphics I remember seeing."

The best riders were sponsored by companies and became "pros". The companies realized that if a skater admired a particular pro they would buy something endorsed by them. "Companies decided that if their boards had the name of their riders on then that would help them sell," says Andy Jenkins, art director of Girl and Chocolate – the twin skateboard companies part owned by filmmaker Spike Jonze. "They started putting out a different pro model every month so they needed more and more graphics and then the symbolism started."

A pro's signature board was meant to reflect his personality, his likes and dislikes. The graphics represented a link between consumers and their idols, allowing them to buy into the dangerous skate lifestyle. "Years ago the graphics had a certain style, or at least people like to think they did," says Jenkins. "Then it was possible to define the aesthetic – it was all skulls and

Once in use, skateboard graphics don't last too long, as can be seen with this before and after shot of a Consolidated board designed by Moish Brenman in 1992. Brenman says: "a board is never finished until it has been skated, worn out and discarded."

punk rock. There was an artist called Pusshead who was really influential. He was a really competent line artist but he just drew skulls. These days the industry's outgrown all that kind of thing and you cannot define the aesthetic quite so easily."

"Skateboarding has a very rich tradition of design that doesn't exactly fit into any category," agrees Todd Francis of Deluxe Distribution. "Skaters really hate being categorized or pigeonholed." These days each company tries to develop its own aesthetic to set its products apart in a crowded market. "The shapes, constructions and manufacturing processes of all skateboards are similar," says Brenman. "The graphics and image of the company are the difference. There are so many companies and so many pros. So many angles have been tried, in the end, all you have to separate you from another company is your graphics."

So what makes a good skateboard graphic? "A good skateboard graphic is anything that will set it apart from the others hanging on the wall of the skate shop," claims Erik Brunetti of Fuct. "If it demands confrontation then it's a good graphic." "A graphic has to have some kind of attitude," agrees Jason Irwin, art director at Acme, "although it depends on the market. If you go for the hardcore skaters then you can maybe use a caricature of Cheech and Chong smoking some big fatty."

Caricatures or rip-offs of celebrities, characters or corporate logos are a familiar part of the skate graphic scene. World Industries, one of the biggest skateboard companies, was one of the first to do it. "Before it was more patterns, plus there was a lot of comic book-style illustration of fighters or cars as well as subculture icons," says World art director John Thomas. "Then when the rave scene started people began to knock off any kind of logo. Our company has always done a lot of spoofs of Disney stuff. You got a cease and desist order and you just say 'OK we'll stop' because you're not doing that one anymore, you've already started on Winnie the Pooh in hell or something. The only time we've had to settle in a lawsuit was when I did Winnie the Pooh with a jar of money instead of honey. Someone nicknamed a workfile Pooh Money. Usually we make a few small changes to the drawing to protect ourselves but because the file name used the word 'Pooh' they got us. Now we're very careful not only with what we use but with how we name it."

"Nothing's sacred," he continues. "If we have an idea then we'll do it and let's see what happens. Even if we do a rip-off we're

thing was skulls which was all about rebellion and taboo, now it's more pop icons and logos – the smiley face meets the devil."

But the rebellious spirit remains. World's devil character was the subject of a mass protest by the far right Christian Coalition when the company included a quasi-religious tract with each board whereby kids could sell their soul to the devil in exchange for a t-shirt. The shirt bore the message "I sold my soul and all I got was this lousy t-shirt".

Unsurprisingly, Fuct's logo and sexual imagery has also attracted many angry letters to the company from outraged parents. As owner and art director Erik Brunetti innocently explains: "They just get bummed out when their kid comes home with a picture of a blow job on his skateboard." Which is just the point.

creatively adding something not just scanning a picture from the video case of some Japanese animation. We're more like Adbusters [the Canadian group which reinterprets commercial messages to make political points about consumerism]."

The ability to respond to, and to send up, figures or events from popular culture is one of skateboarding's most appealing facets. It can do so because of the speed with which new models come and go. "We have 15 pros and each one has two models out at any one time, they overlap, and we change them every two or three months," explains Andy Jenkins. "This year we'll produce at least 150 designs. There's no time to sit and think – we'll spend maybe one or two days on a design. Mostly it's hand-drawn then scanned into a computer to be separated. Usually we silk screen although occasionally we use a UV laminated four colour process, but we don't do it often because the skaters don't like the feel it gives the boards. It's weird because the graphics actually help the performance of the board. Silk screening makes it nice and slick. The more ink on there the better."

Jenkins asked children's book illustrator J. Otto Seibold to design a board for him, but the vast majority of boards are produced by designers who skate themselves – many of them ex-pros. Due to the state of the market they are having to produce designs at an ever-faster rate. "Before now boards had a longer selling period, they could be on the shelves for several months. Now a graphic turns over almost in a month," says John Thomas. "The trend is for really simple bold icons or characters. Our devil character's really taken over. The look is borderline cute but still mysterious. In the mid-80s the big

Early Powell Peralta skateboards.
Far left: Bright Lite, 1980
Left: Beamer, 1979.
Type and logos by Michael Burridge,
art directed by George Powell and
Stacy Peralta

Roskopp V
by Jim Phillips
for Santa Cruz, 1989

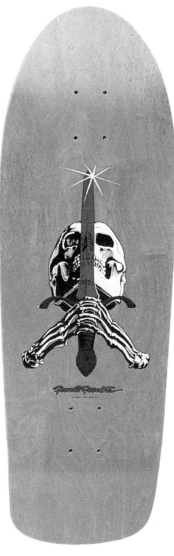

Roskopp Face
by Jim Phillips
for Santa Cruz, 1987

Dodo Skull,
Jason Lee pro model
by Marc McKee
for Blind, 1991

McGill pro model
by Vernon Courtlandt Johnson
for Powell Peralta, 1987

Vernon Courtlandt Johnson
for Powell Peralta, 1990

Brian Krezel
for Maple, 1997

Roskopp Eye
by Jim Phillips
for Santa Cruz, 1989

Brian Krezel
for Maple, 1997

Todd Francis
for Anti Hero, 1995

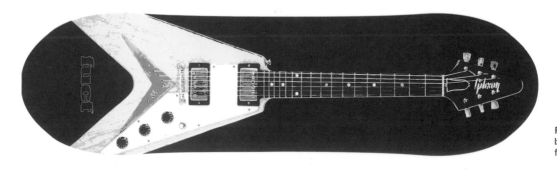

Flying V
by Erik Brunetti
for Fuct, 1996

Slasher, inspired by
Ed "Big Daddy" Roth,
by Jim Phillips
for Santa Cruz, 1988

Caballero pro model
by VCJ
for Powell Peralta, 1987

Vernon Courtlandt Johnson
for Powell Peralta, 1995

Sean Cliver
for Powell Peralta, 1991

McGill pro model
by John Keester
for Powell Peralta, 1990

Mike Lesage
for Think, 1996

**Matt Reason pro model
by Mike Lesage
for Adrenalin, 1996**
Detail

**Kali
by Misha Hollenbach
and Erik Brunetti
for Fuct, 1996**

**Matt Reason pro model by
Mike Lesage for Adrenalin,
1996**

**Brian Krezel
for Maple, 1997**

Randy Colvin pro model
by Marc McKee
for World Industries, 1992
This board prompted a
cease and desist order
from lawyers representing
L. Ron Hubbard's Dianetics
organization

Blackout
by Christian Cooper
for Real, 1996

Jovontae Turner pro model
by Marc McKee
for World Industries, 1992
Obviously a big
banana eater

Adrenalin team board
by Mike Lesage, 1996
Graphic appropriated
from the US dollar

Real Thing
by Deluxe Distribution
art department
for Real, 1996
Any resemblance to
a certain soft drink
is purely intentional

Deeds
by Deluxe Distribution art
department for Real, 1995
Graphic adapted from
the logo of heavy metal
band AC/DC

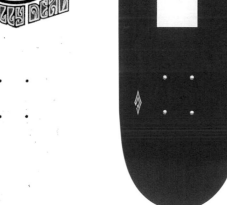

Goodwill Graphics
Randy Colvin pro model
by Marc McKee
for World Industries, 1992
"I thought it was funny that
we got a nasty cease and
desist order from an
organization called
Goodwill," says McKee

Mike Lesage
for Think, 1996
Caustic comment on the
death of Grateful Dead
frontman Jerry Garcia

George Powell
for Powell Peralta, 1995

Black Eye Kid
Jeremy Klein pro model
by Marc McKee
for World Industries, 1991
Shades of Norman
Rockwell

Jeron Wilson pro model
by Andy Jenkins
for Girl, 1996

Burger Board
Jason Lee pro model
by Marc McKee
for Blind, 1991
Betraying Lee's
hamburger of choice

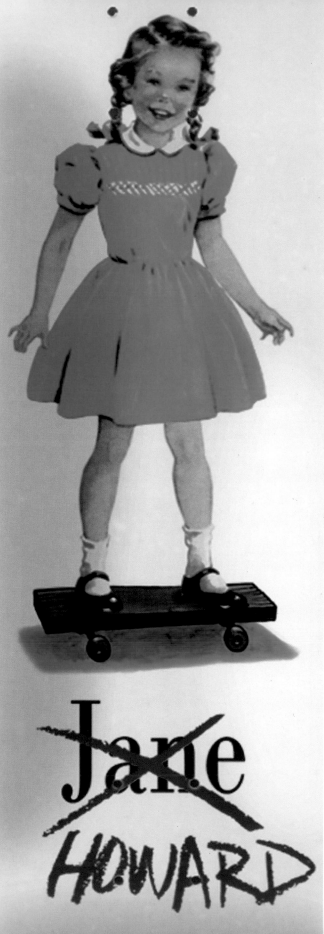

Rick Howard pro boards
by Andy Jenkins
for Girl, 1996
Dick and Jane are American
children's reading book
characters: probably the first
time they've skateboarded

Sean Sheffey pro board
art directed by Rick Howard
for Girl, 1996
The found artwork comes
from a turn-of-the-century
soap advertisement

Peter
by Erik Brunetti
for Fuct, 1996
Tribute to Kiss rock
star Peter Criss

Frankie Hill pro board
by Sean Cliver
for Powell Peralta, 1991
The man with no name

The Devil and Jayne Mansfield
Guy Mariano pro model
by Marc McKee
for Blind, 1994
Alludes to the grisly death of
film star Jayne Mansfield

The Ron Chatman Experience
Ron Chatman pro model
by Marc McKee
for World Industries, 1990
Tribute to Jimi Hendrix
Experience album cover

**Matt Pailes pro board
by Mike Lesage
for Think, 1996**
Controversial movie
A Clockwork Orange
holds obvious attractions
for a young skater

**Conklin pro model
by Sean Cliver
for Powell Peralta, 1991**
Daddy's home!

**1984
Steve Rocco pro model
by Marc McKee for World
Industries, 1992**
A rare literary reference

**Fonseca pro model
by Todd Francis
for Real, 1996**
And a rare touch of
socialist realism

**Girl and Robot
101 team board
by Marc McKee, 1995**

**Planet of the Apes
series by Erik Brunetti
for Fuct, 1992**
These boards are now
collectors' items, often
changing hands for
over $300 each

Chris Branagh pro model
by Marc McKee
for World Industries, 1992
All boards on this spread
pay unlicensed tribute to
favourite Warner Bros
cartoon characters

Dune pro model
by Marc McKee
for World Industries, 1992

Rudy Johnson pro model
by Marc McKee
for Blind, 1992

Jordan Richter pro model
by Marc McKee
for Blind, 1992

Jason Lee pro model
by Marc McKee
for Blind, 1992

Henry Sanchez pro model
by Marc McKee
for Blind, 1993
"It was only available for
a very limited run because
of the danger we might
get sued," says McKee

Kris Markovich pro model
by Marc McKee
for 101, 1992

Steve Rocco pro model
by Marc McKee
for World Industries, 1989
McKee: "We didn't get into
any trouble for using
Winnie the Pooh, but years
later, when we put it on a
snowboard, we got sued."

Chris Pastras pro model
by Christian Cooper
for Stereo, 1996

Spiderman board
by Mike Lesage
for Think, 1996

Velvet Safari
Randy Colvin pro model
by Marc McKee for World
Industries, 1991
This board was covered
in the fuzzy black material
which is used as hair on
GI Joe dolls

Jesus
Gabriel Rodriguez pro model
by Marc McKee
for 101, 1992

Sean Young pro model
by Todd Francis
for Anti Hero, 1996

Blind team board
by Marc McKee, 1997

Buddha with Slurpee
Eric Koston pro model
by Marc McKee
for 101, 1993

Accidental Gun Death
Guy Mariano pro model
by Marc McKee
for Blind, 1992

Stuffed Animal Murder
Adam McNatt
pro model
by Sean Cliver
for 101, 1992

"A LOT OF TIMES GUYS WOULD BRING IN THINGS FROM COMIC BOOKS. ONCE WE TOOK A PHOTO FROM LIFE MAGAZINE THAT SHOWED A CAT THAT GOT HIT BY A CAR AND THERE WAS THIS LITTLE GIRL STANDING RIGHT NEXT TO IT WITH A TOY GUN IN HER HAND — IT LOOKED LIKE SHE'D SHOT THE CAT ."

Mike Lesage, former art director Think and Adrenalin

Paul Zuanich pro model
by Mike Lesage
for Think, 1996

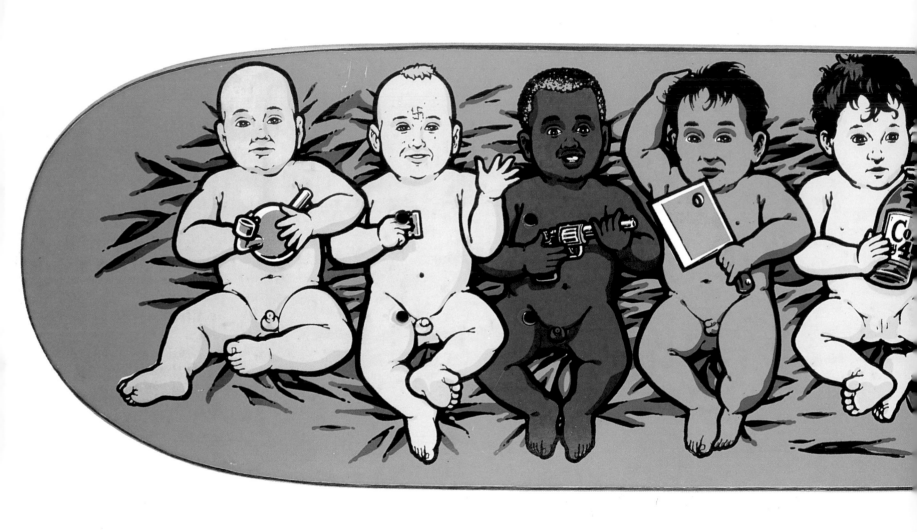

Adam McNatt pro model
by Sean Cliver
for 101, 1995

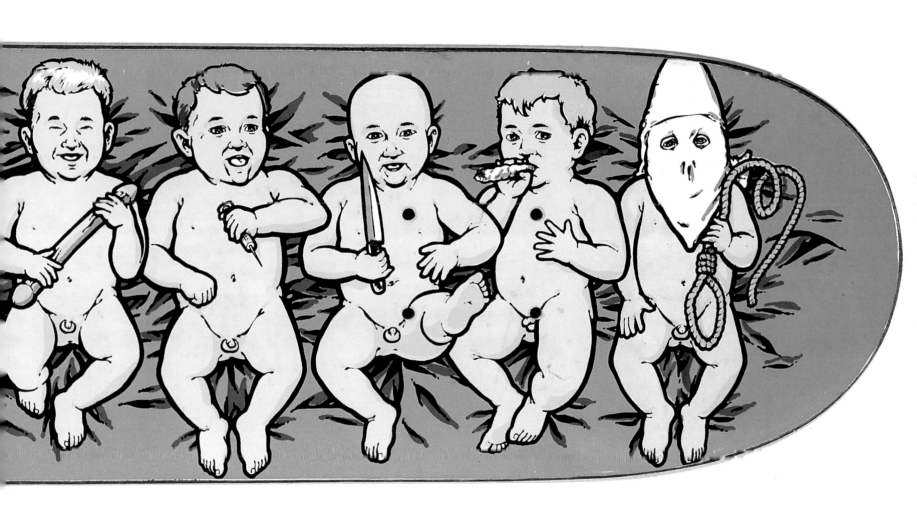

REAR-END RUDY

Pro models for, from left, Jordan Richter, Guy Mariano, Rudy Johnson and Henry Sanchez by Marc McKee for Blind, 1992 This series sends up the Garbage Pail Kids series of trading cards. Each board came with a set of four trading cards

Devil Man Face
by Marc McKee
for World Industries, 1996
This little devil has become
the best-selling character
in skateboarding

Marc McKee
for World Industries, 1996

Marc McKee
for World Industries, 1996

Marc McKee
for World Industries, 1996

Daredevil Laughing Face
by Moish Brenman for
Consolidated, 1992

MATT
PAILES

Fat America
Kris Markovich pro model
by Sean Cliver
for Prime, 1995

American Icons
Jason Lee pro board
by Marc McKee
for Blind, 1991

Matt Pailes pro board
by Mike Lesage
for Think, 1996

Horned Hand
by Erik Brunetti
for Fuct, 1996

CAINE GAYLE

PRIME

Prime

PRIME

PRIMI

Prime team boards
by Sean Cliver, 1996

Top:
Max Schaaf pro board
by Todd Francis
for Real, 1996

Middle:
Misha Hollenbach
and Erik Brunetti
for Fuct, 1996

Above:
Shiloh Greathouse pro model
by Marc McKee
for World Industries, 1996
Greathouse's graffiti tag is Hyst

Challenger
Natas Kaupas pro model
by Marc McKee
for 101, 1992
Lichtenstein-style illustration
of the Challenger space
shuttle disaster

Crash
Dave Leamon
for Acme, 1996

Mike Lesage
for Think, 1996

Mike Lesage
for Think, 1996

Chupacabra
by Dave Leamon
for Acme, 1996
Inspired by news
stories of a
mythical beast
of the same name
attacking farm
animals in Mexico

Jason Noto
for Think, 1996

Crossing Guard
Daewon Song
pro model
by Marc McKee
for World Industries,
1995

OC Bladerunners
Danny Way
pro model
by Marc McKee
for Blind, 1991
Features portraits
of Way's pro
teammates

Bar Scene
by Dave Leamon
for Acme, 1996

Freak Show
by Dave Leamon
for Acme, 1996

Harem
Steve Rocco
pro model
by Marc McKee
for World Industries,
1992

A Skater
by Dan Pinosian
for Acme, 1996

Adrenalin team board
by Mike Lesage, 1996

Invisible team board
by Linda Prettyman, 1997

Acme team board
by Dave Leamon,
1996

Adrenalin team board
by Mike Lesage, 1996

Brian Young pro model for Invisible,
Dave Mayhew pro models for Maple,
all by Brian Krezel, 1997

BRIAN YOUNG

DAVE MAYHEW

DAVE MAYHEW

MAYHEW

All boards this page
by Ren & Stimpy creator
John Kricfalusi
for Formula One,
art director Jason Irwin,
1996

Cheerleader
Karma Tsocheff pro
model by Moish Brenman
for Consolidated, 1993

Ronnie Creager pro model
by Jay Bryan
for Blind, 1996

Gideon Choi pro model
by Jay Bryan
for Blind, 1996

Blind team board
by Jay Bryan/
John Thomas, 1996

John Kricfalusi for
Formula One, art
director Jason Irwin,
1996

Tim Gavin pro model
by Shawn Cassidy
for Girl, 1995

Eric Koston pro model
by Mel Bend
for Girl, 1995

Fonseca pro model
by Mark Gonzales
for Real, 1997

Carl Shipman pro model
by Christian Cooper
for Stereo, 1996

Guy Mariano pro model
by Clive Noctchaw
for Girl, 1996

Sean Sheffey
pro model
by Bucky Fukumoto
for Girl, 1996

Guy Mariano
pro model
by J. Otto Seibold
for Girl, 1996

Chico Brenes
pro model
by Mel Bend
for Chocolate, 1997

Gino Iannucci
pro model
by Geoff McFetridge
for Chocolate, 1997

Keenan Milton
pro model
by Geoff McFetridge
for Chocolate, 1997

From left:
Mike Carroll,
Rudy Johnson
and Rick Howard
pro models
by Mel Bend
for Girl, 1997

Vinnie Ponte pro model
by Dave Kinsey
for Tree Fort, 1996

Alphonzo Rawls pro board
by Dave Kinsey
for Tree Fort, 1996

Fire Fighter
by Dave Kinsey
for Tree Fort, 1996

Ronnie Bongo
by Dave Kinsey
for Tree Fort, 1996

Bug
by Dave Kinsey
for Tree Fort, 1996

In the event of a loss of cabin pressure masks supplying Nitrous Oxide will release from the overhead panel. Place the mask securely over your face and breath deeply to relieve the stress of impending death.

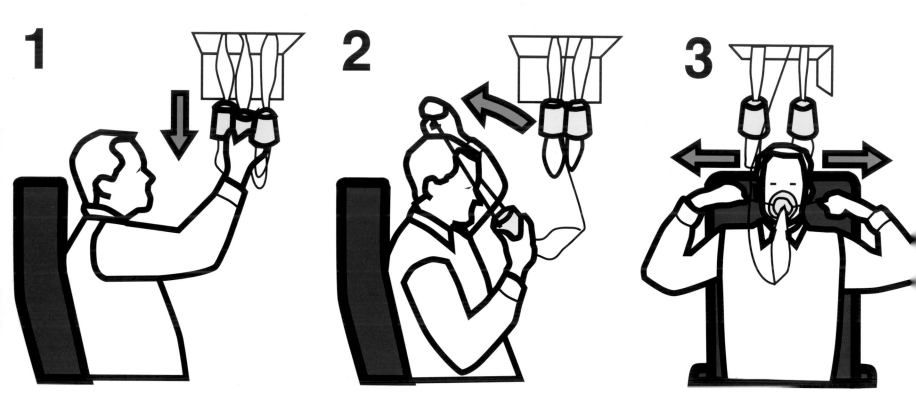

Jason Irwin
for Formula One,
1996

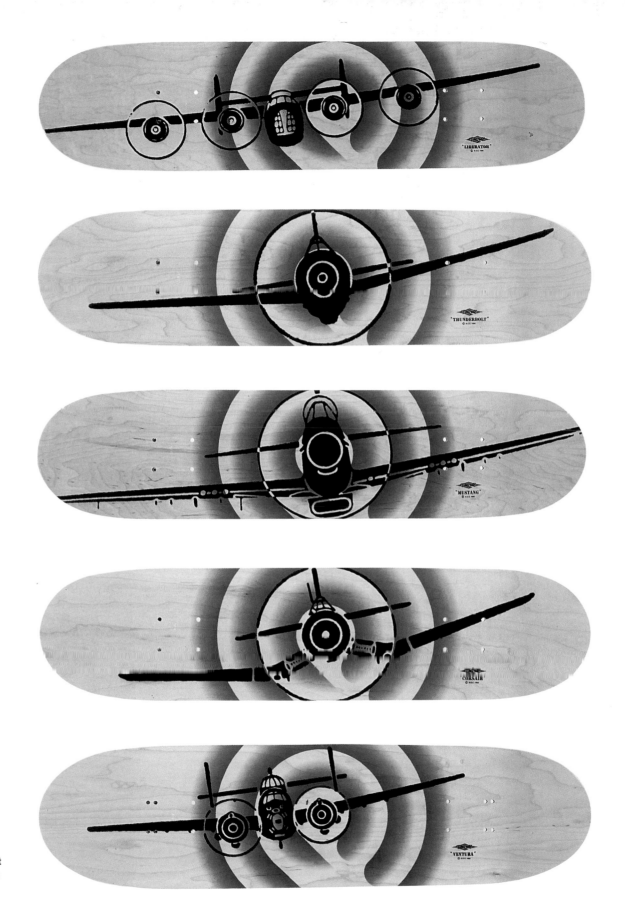

Jim Knight
for Powell,
1995

Menace team board
by Robert Mars/
John Thomas,
1997

Subliminal team board
by Shep Fairey, 1997

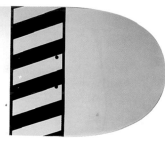

Excavator
Karma Tsocheff pro model
by Moish Brenman
for Consolidated, 1995
One of the Construction
series. Each board came
with a leaflet on how to
build a skatepark

Doug Saenz pro model
by Moish Brenman
for Consolidated, 1995

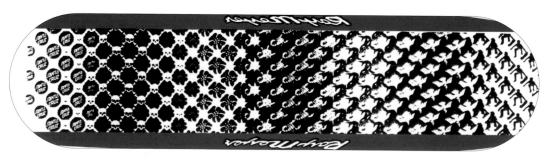

Ray Meyer pro model
by Jim Phillips
for Santa Cruz, 1989
Inspired by Escher's
Metamorphosis

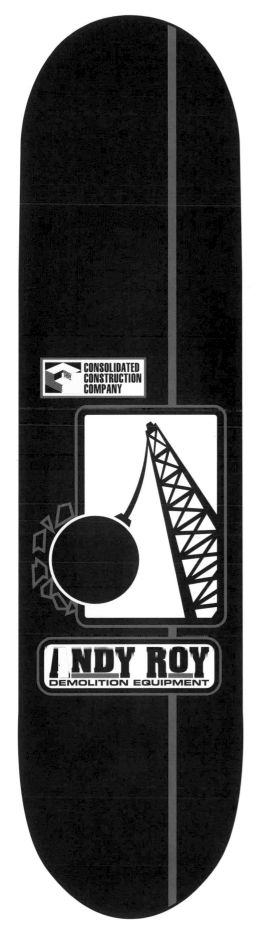

**Andy Roy pro models
by Moish Brenman for
Consolidated, 1995**
More in the
Construction series

Shep Fairey, 1996
Fairey's Andre the Giant is a familiar graffiti character featuring on fly posters pasted up all over the USA

Keenan Milton pro model by Andy Jenkins for Chocolate, 1996

Jason Irwin for Acme, 1997
The artwork is composed of a series of prints based on the lives of the saints which Irwin found in his parents' loft

Mike Carroll pro model, found artwork, art directed by Andy Jenkins for Girl, 1995

Left to right:
**Guy Mariano, Rick Howard,
Mike Carroll and Eric Koston
pro models photographed
by Spike Jonze, art directed
by Andy Jenkins for Girl, 1995**
The characters in the pictures
are the pros themselves in heavy
make-up. This style was also
used by Jonze in a series of
pictures of band the Beastie Boys

Flow2 series, Koston pro model
by Michael Leon for Girl, art
director Andy Jenkins, 2002

Flow2 series, McCrank pro model
by Rob Abeyta Jr for Girl, art
director Andy Jenkins, 2002

Flow2 series, Anderson pro model
by Michael Leon for Girl, art
director Andy Jenkins, 2002

Elvira series, art director/
illustrator Fernando Elvira
for Cliché, 2002

Wooden OG series Anderson pro model by Michael Leon for Girl, art director Andy Jenkins, 2002

Wooden OG series Howard pro model by Andy Jenkins for Girl, art director Andy Jenkins, 2002

Wooden OG series Johnson pro model by Rob Abeyta Jr for Girl, art director Andy Jenkins, 2002

Wooden OG series Mariano pro model by Andy Mueller for Girl, art director Andy Jenkins, 2002

Wooden OG series Sheffey pro model by Andy Jenkins for Girl, art director Andy Jenkins, 2002

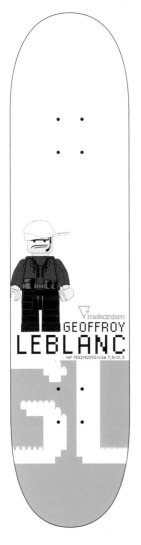

Geoffroy LeBlanc pro model by Sebastian Caldas for Mekanism, 2002

From Thai series by Pawel Kozlowski for Popular, 2002

Calendar series Daclin pro model by Eric Frenay for Cliché, 2002

Daclin pro model by Pawel Kozlowski for Cliché, 2002

OG series Johnson pro model by Andy Jenkins for Girl, art director Andy Jenkins, 2001

Suski Lite,
illustrator Mark Nardelli,
art director Steve Rodriguez
for 5boro, 2002

Metromob series
Hamburg by Marcnesium
for Hessenmob, 2000

Metromob series
Dresden by Gresce
for Hessenmob, 2002

Experiments in Truth series
Bird by Don Pendelton
for Hessenmob, 2001

Wall1
by Eric Frenay
for Wall Street, 2002

Flow2 series Howard
pro model by Tony Larson
for Girl, art director Andy Jenkins,
2002

Flow2 series Carroll
pro model by Tony Larson for Girl,
art director Andy Jenkins, 2002

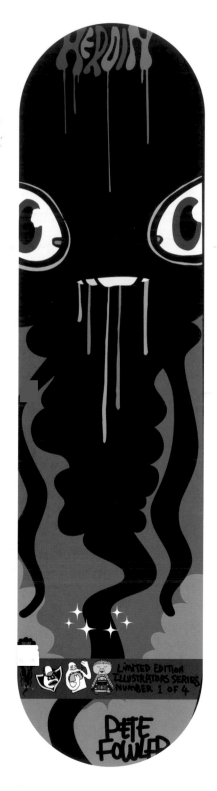

Heroin Illustrators series by (left
to right) Pete Fowler, James Jarvis,
Mark Foster, Simon True, 2002

Proposals for skateboard series
by Peter Stemmler, Eboy, 2002

GUY MARIANO

ERIC KOSTON

RICK HOWARD

COLIN MCKAY

TONY FERGUSON

Modern Chair series,
all by Tony Larson
for Girl, 2000

JERON WILSON

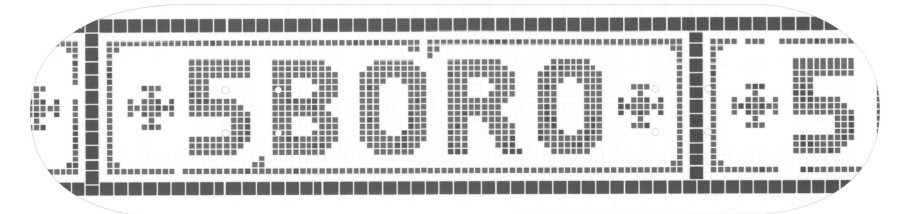

Top to bottom:
Skyline, Interlock (both illustrated by
Mark Nardelli) and Mosaic (illustrated
by Alexander Eben Meyer), all art directed
by Steve Rodriguez for 5boro, 2002

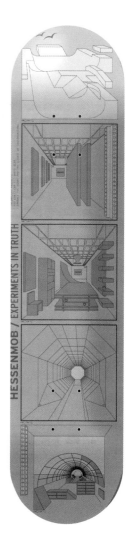

Modern Sign series McKay
pro model by Tony Larson
for Girl, art director Andy Jenkins,
2002

Modern Sign series Johnson
pro model by Tony Larson
for Girl, art director Andy Jenkins,
2002

Metromob series
Warsaw
by Pawel Kozlowski
for Hessenmob, 2002

Metromob series
London
by Henry Obasi for
Hessenmob, 2002

Experiments in Truth series
Stacked
by Michael Leon
for Hessenmob, 2001

SNOW

Snowboarding has to be the world's trendiest sport. It is everywhere: in commercials, in pop promos, magazines and fashion shoots. Sponsors are queuing up to grab some reflected glory, pushing earnings for the top pros beyond $200,000 a year – which is not too bad for a teenager.

As a result, as explained in the introduction to this book, snowboarding has aroused resentment, even derision from practitioners of other board sports. It has been accused by jealous rivals of being a Johnny-come-lately, lacking a culture of its own, stealing unashamedly from surfing and from skateboarding. But many of those who initially took up snowboarding were already either surfing or skateboarding, so it is not surprising that in the early days of the late 1980s snowboarding looked to them for a cultural lead. "Snowboarding is the mountain kids' version of surfing. It gave them their own cool thing," says John Thomas of World Industries. "But the attitude comes from skating. They were outlaws just like skaters, because they weren't allowed on the snow."

The mountain slopes became battle-grounds as angry skiers complained that snowboarders ruined the piste when they carved out their turns. "Back in the early days snowboarders hated skiers and vice versa," claims Robynne Raye of Seattle's Modern Dog design consultancy which has been creating graphics for K2 snowboards since 1991. But many of the first snowboards borrowed graphics from skiing or other established action sports. The look was simple, brightly-coloured and logo-orientated.

It seemed as though the manufacturers did not understand who these young new customers were and did not know how to appeal to them – especially the many ski companies which were seeking to cross over. "A lot of snowboarders thought K2 was a phony company because it made skis," says Raye. "The same designers did both so you had these 40, 50 year-old art directors trying to do what they thought 22 year-olds would find hip and they talked down to them. Eventually K2 snowboards broke away from the ski side and set up in a separate building to do its own thing."

Designers borrowed freely from surfing and skateboarding, recognizing kindred spirits, but as the market began to mature, snowboarding started to develop its own graphic language. Muted, grungy colours and baggy clothing contrasted to the bright, cheery world of skiing and allowed snowboarders to express their separate identity on the slopes. Scott Clum's work for Morrow from the early 1990s, for example, features dark, distressed imagery more akin to a Nirvana album cover than a healthy leisure pursuit. "Snowboarding wasn't a glamour thing back then, it was very spontaneous and underground, kind of down and dirty," he explains. "I was trying to develop its own culture by introducing its own art into the catalogues and boards. We were trying to get over the feeling, the vibe."

However, snowboarding became a victim of its own success and soon found itself having to cater for a wider audience. "At first it was much more of a subculture but there are lots of different types of people snowboarding now," says Raye. "You've got women, moms, their kids – the market is huge and the whole industry has begun to take itself a lot more seriously." In response to an entirely different target market the graphics had to change. Boards are now sold in conservative ski shops to an increasingly wealthy and older clientele. The competition is fierce and the consequences of failure much greater. "Retailers are a conservative lot, but especially so in a market as volatile as snowboards," says Richard Green of Morrow's in-house design department. "The willingness to take risks is shared only by those who are prepared to be here today and gone tomorrow. In 1996 there were around 450 snowboard companies. In 1997 that came down by almost half."

Now, unlike surfboards or skateboards, snowboard companies put new boards through months of market research before bringing out their new lines each autumn. "Boards can take at least six months, often nine months," says David Covell of JDK, Burton's design company. "We start with round table discussions with our riders where everyone brings in scrapbooks of ideas." Once a shortlist is thrashed out, opinions will be sought from the company's sales team and prominent retailers.

"It can be an excruciating process getting to the final board," says Raye. "We work a year ahead and it's not easy trying to predict what a 22 year-old will find hip in 12 months' time. We might do 50 designs for one board with changes of colour or logo placement. We hand over our design to the in-house design department and they'll maybe print up one or two to get feedback.

Occasionally things get changed without our consultation. Sometimes they'll even axe the whole thing two weeks before shipping."

Designers work to the shape of the board, allowing for the position of the rider's feet and any necessary cropping. "There's nothing really confining about the shape," says Clum. "But you have to be careful when you're doing graphics for the base because the material can vary in density and you're never sure what's going to show." The introduction of dye sublimation printing processes has allowed designers to use infinite amounts of colour and produces sharper, brighter results but Clum, for one, misses the old method of screen printing where each colour was printed separately. "I really use to get off on the feeling of the ink. Now 80 per cent of boards are dye sublimated and I think it's really cold. I don't like that look at all. It's like taking straight art, beating it to death and sticking it on a board. I want to see that separated colour and feel the inks on the board."

The introduction of dye sublimation has coincided with a return to a brighter, primary colour palette partly encouraged by the amount of ski companies crossing over into this lucrative market. "A lot of ski companies are getting involved to try and say 'we're hip' but then there's also a niche for hardcore skater graphics – the two types of company are coming from opposite sides and in the middle you've got wholly snowboard companies like Burton or Morrow who can have a sort of surfy look or something like the work of [ex-Ray Gun designer] David Carson," says Thomas.

The result is a snowboarding scene which, graphically, has something for everyone. "It's the full jambalaya, the full mix," says Thomas. "You can have the craziest, bad cartoons but then there are ten million people trying to do variations on racing stripes. You've got beautiful, sublimated, full illustrations but then the same company will put Beavis and Butthead on a board." As a reaction to all this graphic choice, many companies have been switching over to simpler designs, encouraging riders to personalize their boards with stickers to ensure that they will not see another one exactly the same out on the slopes.

"There are so many snowboard companies now it's hard to find a unique look," admits Jeff Bartel, Morrow's current art director, "but it's very challenging to try and appeal to everybody. It's a great canvas for a designer to work on."

Indeed, many designers have realized that snowboards represent an excellent opportunity for graphic expression. Some of graphic design's biggest names have designed for snowboards. Neville Brody has created a logo for Salomon, David Carson was art director for Burton for a time and Carlos Segura has designed graphics for XXX Snowboards for several years.

"K2 is a highly-coveted client," says Robynne Raye. "A lot of design firms seek out snowboard companies because they are willing to take risks and they see the boards and catalogues and ads picking up all sorts of awards. We've certainly gotten a lot of attention because of the work we do for K2. It's led to other jobs because people want to buy in that attitude."

Snowboards offer designers the chance to create high-profile, mass-market objects for a young, style-led clientele to a comparatively loose brief allowing for a comparatively large amount of artistic licence. And, statistically, the work has a great chance of winning industry awards. As Raye says: "It's like a designer's dream job."

The sport embodies all those elusive elements of cool that marketers and media people find so attractive – young people, rebellion, exotic locations, great clothes, exciting action, slang, music. Its spirituality made it ideal for the 1990s, combining surfing's sense of proximity to nature with the hard-edged cynicism of skateboarding. Advertisers looking for a shortcut to street credibility find it irresistible – it is dangerous but it is not immediately threatening. Unsurprisingly, MTV has bought into snowboarding in a big way. The only worry seems to be whether the sport's rich visual language will cope with the encroachment of commercialism. If it becomes too popular, the young people who are the sport's lifeblood will abandon it for a new thrill, and what were once canvases for the expression of a subculture may become mere consumer goods packaging.

But the signs are good. Despite its huge global popularity, surfing has maintained its ability to provide vivid, exciting graphics with a strong streak of personalization and has kept its street credibility largely intact. Skateboarding, too, provides inspiration, surviving as it did the potentially fatal embarrassment of having been a 1970s fad. If those two sports can come through with an aesthetic that remains inspiring and influential then so can snowboarding. As with all subcultures, its fate rests with the committed few who will be prepared to keep going when the enthusiasm of others has begun to flag – and when MTV's cameras have been turned elsewhere.

"KILL YOUR SKIS."

T-shirt slogan

Fatbob
by Vittorio Costarella,
Modern Dog for K2,
1992

HC Snowboard
by Michael
Strassburger and
Robynne Raye,
Modern Dog for K2,
1992

Rally Sport
by Vittorio Costarella,
Modern Dog for K2, 1995

JuJu Snowboard
by Vittorio Costarella,
Modern Dog for K2,
1993

Eldorado
by Vittorio Costarella,
Modern Dog for K2,
1996

Fatbob
by George Estrada,
Modern Dog for K2,
1995

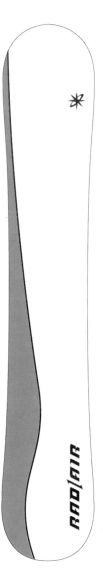

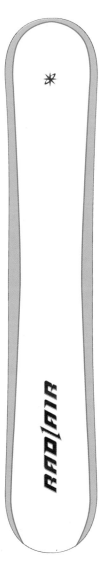

Dart
by Vittorio Costarella,
Modern Dog for K2,
1995

AC Snowboard
by Michael Strassburger
and Vittorio Costarella,
Modern Dog for K2, 1992

Tanker 162
by Marcel Langenegger
for Rad/Air, 1997

Tanker 172
by Marcel Langenegger
for Rad/Air, 1997

Tanker 182
by Marcel Langenegger
for Rad/Air, 1997

Hornet, base
by Uccio Demirci
for Rad/Air,
1997/98

From top:
Charge 164, Charge 152,
Ranger 149, Circuit 154,
Charge 161, Charge 155
by Carlos Segura
for XXX Snowboards, 1996

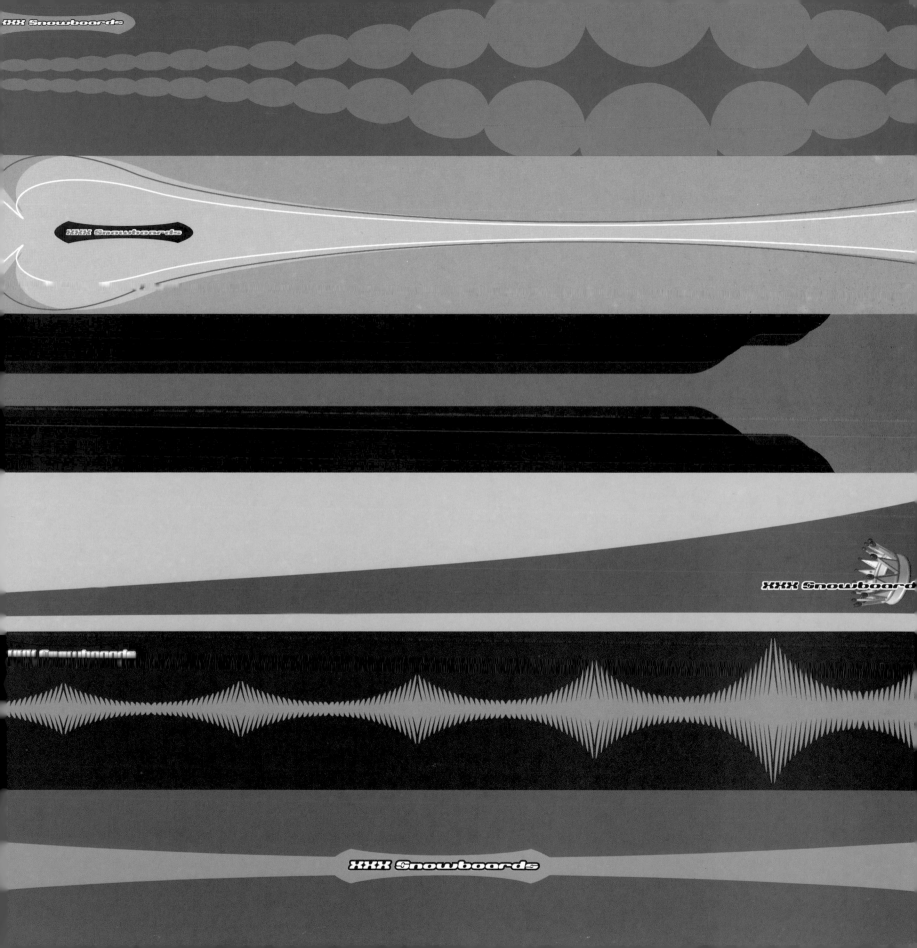

Nova Freestyle
by Mike Dawson
for Nitro, 1997/98

Hazard Freestyle
by Mike Dawson
for Nitro, 1997/98

Grom Kids
by Mike Dawson
for Nitro, 1997/98

Hazard Freestyle, base
by Mike Dawson
for Nitro, 1997/98

Spirit Freestyle, base
by Mike Dawson
for Nitro, 1997/98

Fatbob
by Vittorio Costarella,
Modern Dog for K2,
1993

Jager DiPaola Kemp
for Burton, 1996

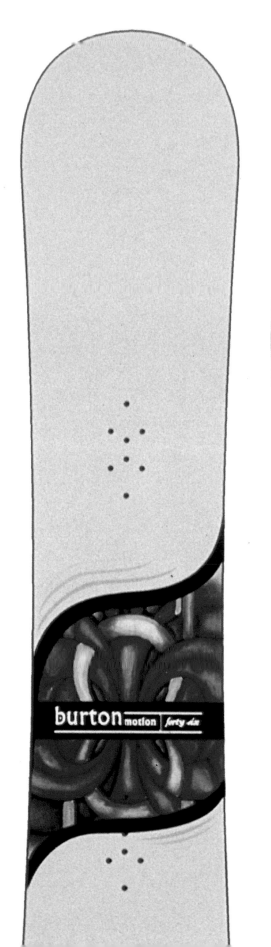

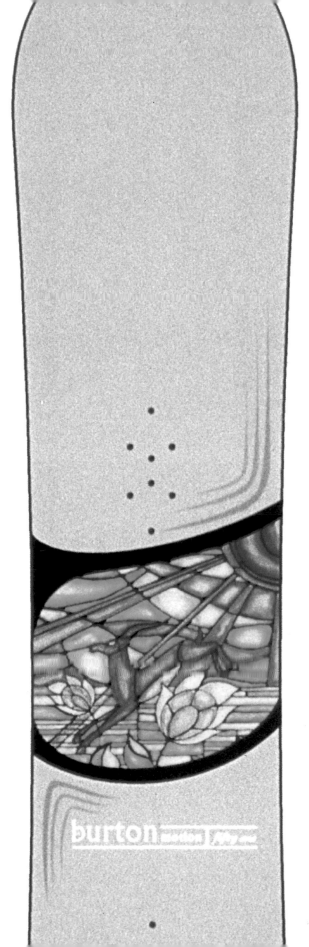

burton motion forty six

burton

burton motion fifty two

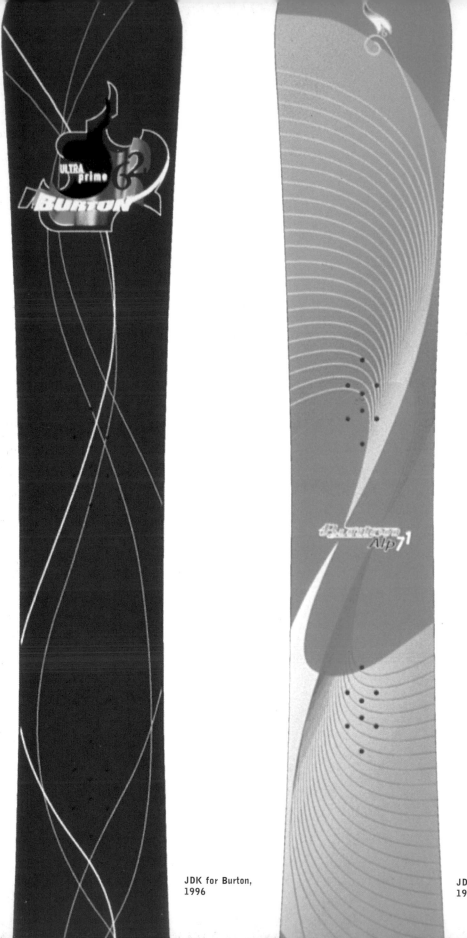
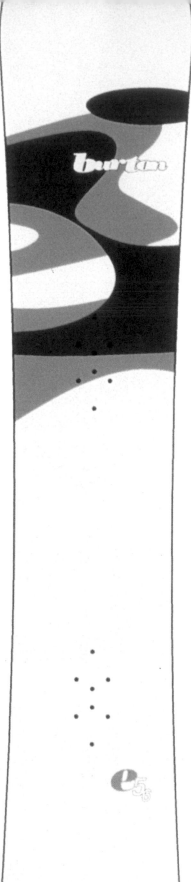

JDK for Burton,
1996

JDK for Burton,
1996

JDK for Burton,
1996

Jamie Lynn pro model,
medium wide base
by Jamie Lynn
for Lib Technologies,
1997

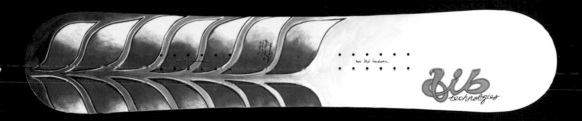

Jamie Lynn pro model,
small narrow top
by Jamie Lynn
for Lib Technologies,
1997

Jamie Lynn pro model,
medium wide top
by Jamie Lynn
for Lib Technologies,
1997

Jamie Lynn pro model,
long top
by Jamie Lynn
for Lib Technologies,
1997

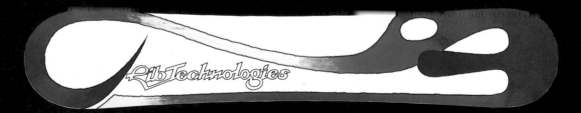

Matt Cummins
pro model, base
by Matt Cummins
for Lib Technologies,
1997

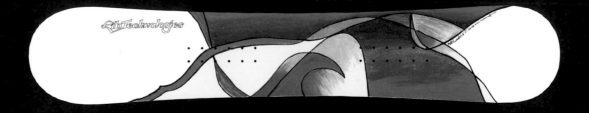

Matt Cummins
pro model, top
by Matt Cummins
for Lib Technologies,
1997

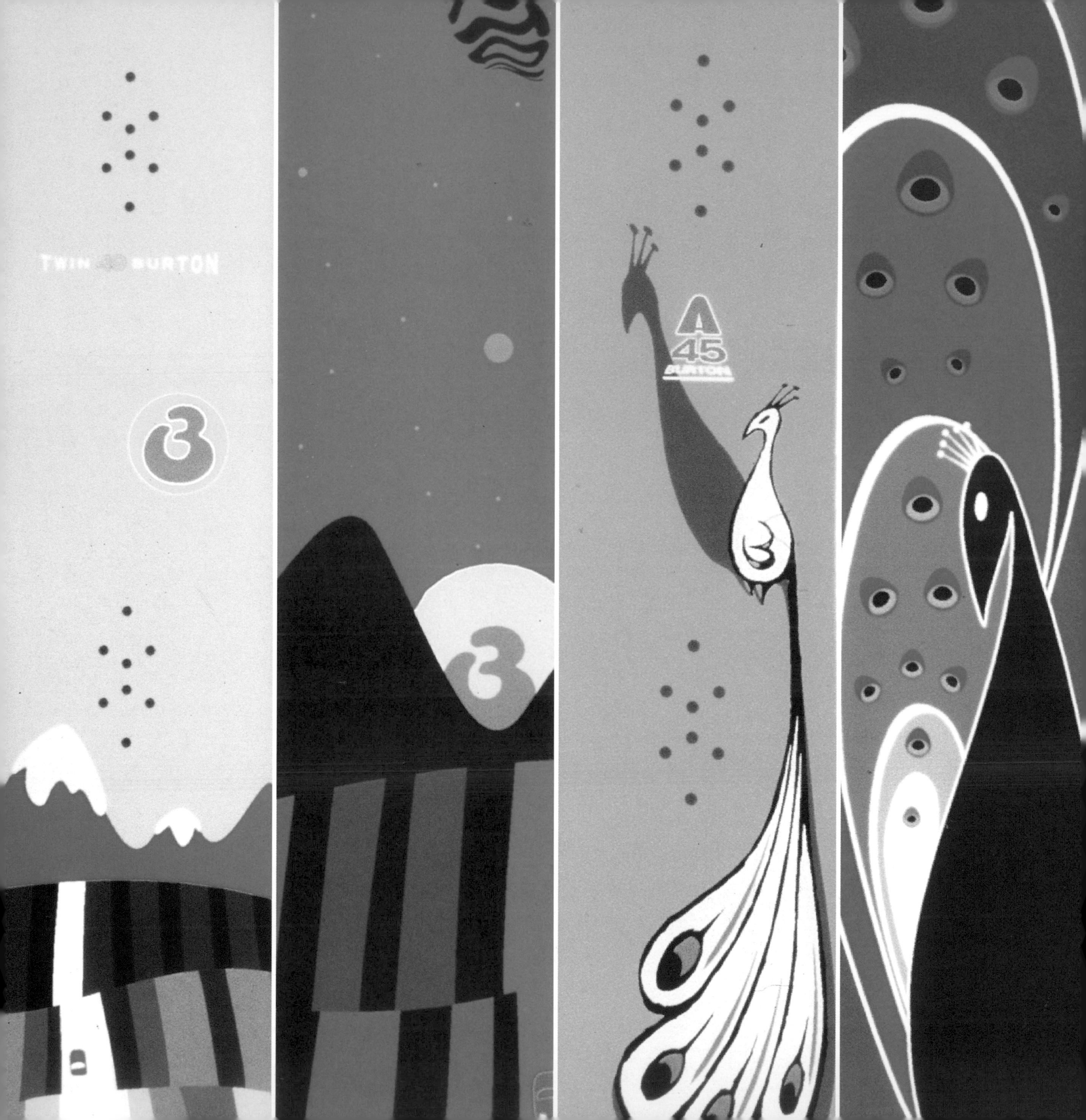
TWIN BURTON
A
45

Following pages:
spreads from
Fanatic
1997/98
catalogue
by 3 De Luxe

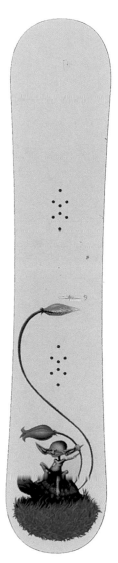

JDK for Burton,
1996

Troll, top
by JDK for Burton,
1996

JDK for Burton,
1996

Neil Harrison and
Mike Dawson for
Nitro, 1997/98

JDK for Burton,
1993

Sea Life, top
JDK for Burton,
1996

From left: Alps top and base
and Peacock top and base
by JDK for Burton, 1996

HOME

HOME 143, 148, 153, 158 IE
HOME JUN. 113, 123, 133

**A PURE FREESTYLEBOARD FOR EXTREME
PIPE RIDING AND BIG AIRS**

FEATURES • true twintip-shape for fakierides and switchstance tricks
• vertical laminated woodcore for perfect flex
• enough sidecut for controlled riding between moves
• short tips for extreme spins; with just the right lift for pipetransition

HOME JUN.

• the boardflex specially trimmed for teh weight
and the demands of the young freestlyrs
• Syncore-Construction

HOME SWEET HOME

Topsheet
Biaxial fabric
Multiaxial fabric
Sidewall
Woodcore beech+poplar
Shockabsorber
Edge
Base

HOME

FARE

DAS ASYMMETRISCHE FREECARVEBOARD FÜR DEN
ALPINORIENTIERTEN FREERIDER,
DER AUF DIE VORZÜGE DER ASYMMETRIE NICHT VERZICHTEN WILL.

FEATURES • asymmetrischer Shape mit Slalomtaillierung
• der asymmetrische, vertikal verleimte Holzkern mit Torsionbox
sorgt für guten Kantengriff und schnellen Kantenwechsel
• ausreichend Nosekick für genug Auftrieb im Powder
• genügend Tailkick für Fakierides und relaxtes all mountain riding

THE FARE IS REAL

Topsheet
Biaxial fabric
Multiaxial fabric
Sidewall
Woodcore beech+poplar
Shockabsorber
Edge
Base

FARE 162, 157, 152

FARE

PLAYER

PLAYER 141, 148, 155, 161

Captopsheet
Biaxial fabric
Multiaxial fabric
Wood-compound-core
Shockabsorber
Edge
Base

ITCS: Intelligent Torsion Control System

FEATURES • directional shape for better turning control
• the new developed Triradialshape for precise softboot carving
• the right waist width for good floating in poeder, ITCS for better edge to edge ability
• more snap in the tail for better ollie ability

PLAYER-SERIES IN FULL-CAP-WOOD-COMPUND-CONSTRUCTION
CRASHES UNKNOWN DIMENSIONS OF ALL MOUNTAIN RIDING FOR FREERIDERS

JUST PLAY WITH IT

PLAYER

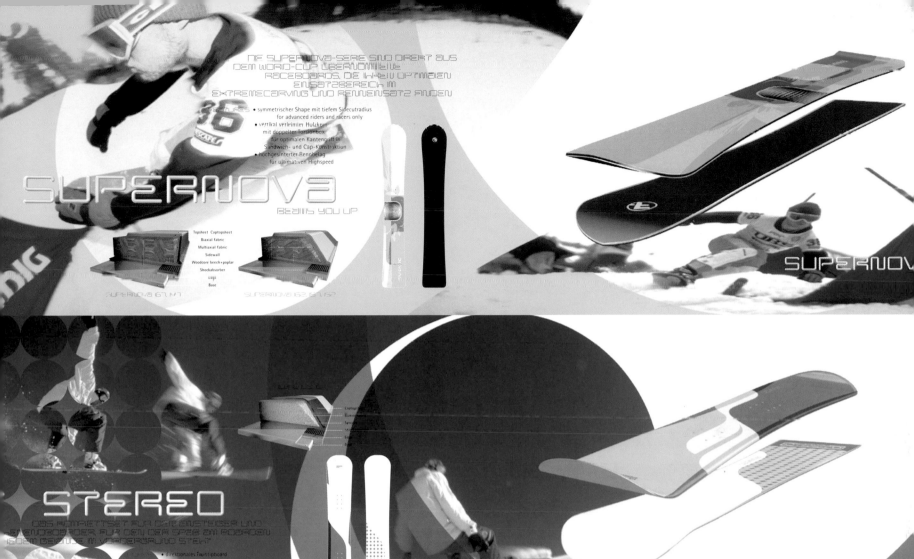

SUPERNOVA

beams you up

DIE SUPERNOVA-SERIE SIND DIREKT AUS
DEM WORLD-CUP ÜBERNOMMENE
RACEBOARDS, DIE IHREN OPTIMALEN
EINSATZBEREICH IM
EXTREMECARVING UND RENNEINSATZ FINDEN

FEATURES • symmetrischer Shape mit tiefem Sidecutradius
for advanced riders and racers only
• vertikal verleimter Holzkern
mit doppelter Torsionbox
für optimalen Kantengriff in
Sandwich- und Cap-Konstruktion
• hochgesinterter Rennbelag
für ultimativen Highspeed

Topsheet Captopsheet
Biaxial fabric
Multiaxial fabric
Sidewall
Woodcore beech+poplar
Shockabsorber
Edge
Base

SUPERNOVA 167, 187   SUPERNOVA 162, 167, 167

SUPERNOVA

STEREO

DAS KOMPLETTSET FÜR DEN EINSTEIGER UND
GELEGENHEITSBOARDER, FÜR DEN DER SPASS AM BOARDEN
BEIM GENUSS IM VORDERGRUND STEHT

• direktionales Twintipboard
• extrem einfache Schwungauslösung
durch weichere Gesamtabstimmung
• die starke Taillierung ermöglicht eine
genaue Schwungsteuerung
• Syncore-Cap Technologie

JUST STEREO

STEREO

CARE

JADE FÜR DEN SPORTLICHEN FREECARVER ENTWICKELT,
MEHR VON SEINEM BOARD VERLANGT ALS CARVEN

Triradialshape: Die Taillierung wird durch 3 unterschiedliche Radien bestimmt

Captopsheet
Biaxial fabric
Multiaxial fabric
Wood-compound-core
Shockabsorber
Edge
Base

• neuentwickelter Triradialshape für exaktes Carving
• Das ITCS ist verantwortlich für optimalen Kantengriff
bei langen Carves
und schnellen Kantenwechsel bei kurzen Slalomturns
• die All-Terrain-Nose und genügend Tailkick setzen dem Board
auch abseits der Piste keine Grenzen
• Full-Cap-Wood-Compound Technologie für leichte und robuste Bauweise

DAS SAHNESTÜCK UNTER DEN FREECARVEBOARDS

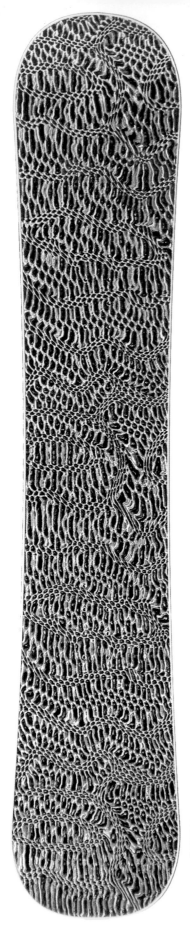

LammBoard, top
by Marcel
Langenegger
for Rad/Air,
1996/97

Allways 154
by Mirko Noser
for Rad/Air,
1997/98

Twin
by JDK
for Burton, 1993

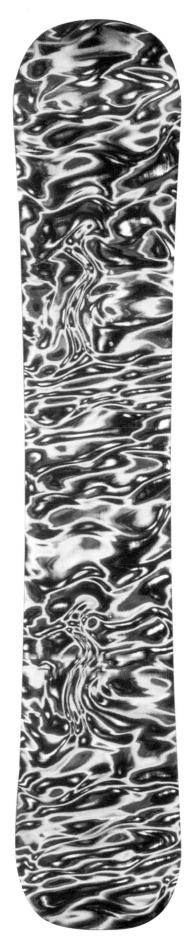

LammBoard
by Marcel
Langenegger
for Rad/Air,
1995/96

LammBoard
by Marcel
Langenegger
for Rad/Air,
1995/96

Super Fly
by Vittorio
Costarella and
Michael
Strassburger,
Modern Dog
for K2, 1995

JDK for Burton,
1994

Twin 47
JDK for Burton,
1993

Tricky Glo
by George Estrada,
Modern Dog for K2,
1996

LammBoard, base
by Marcel
Langenegger
for Rad/Air,
1996/97

Fatbob, base
by George Estrada,
Modern Dog for K2,
1994

Facing page, left to right:
Indi, base by Marcel Langenegger; Sport, base;
Allways, top; Sport, top all by Mirko Noser
for Rad/Air, 1997/98

ALLWAYS 154

RAD AIR

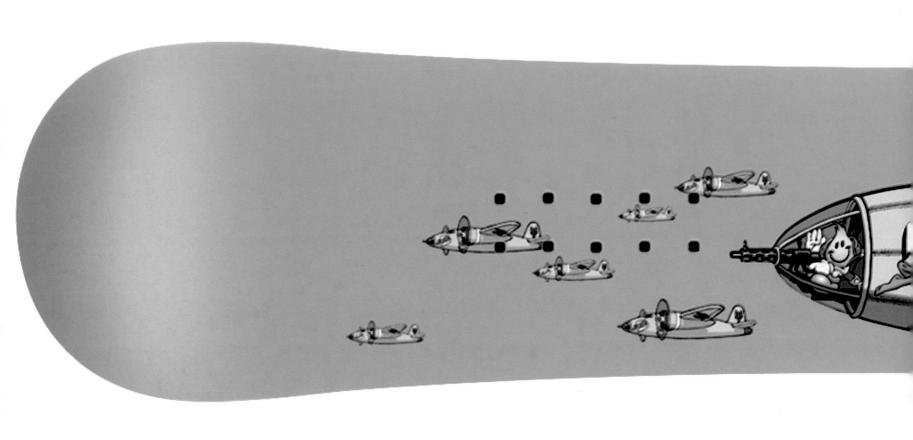

Marc McKee
for World Industries,
1996

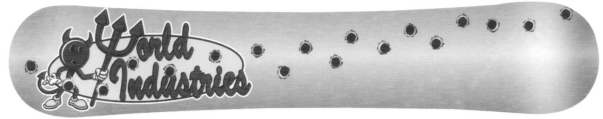

Marc McKee
for World Industries,
1996

Emmagator, base
by Nick Russian
for Lib Technologies,
1997

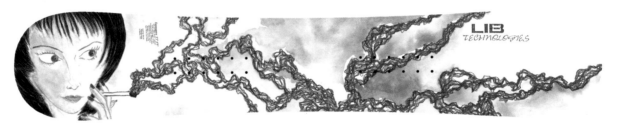

Emmagator, top
by Nick Russian
for Lib Technologies,
1997

Emma, base
by Nick Russian
for Lib Technologies,
1997

Emma, top
by Nick Russian
for Lib Technologies,
1997

El Limbo
by Vittorio
Costarella, Modern
Dog for K2, 1995

Kook
by Vittorio Costarella,
Modern Dog for K2,
1995

Squid
by Vittorio Costarella,
Modern Dog for K2,
1995

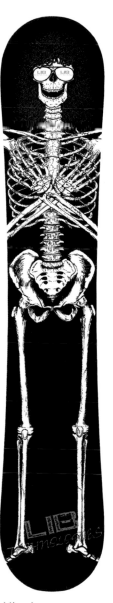

Litagator
by Mark Gale
for Lib Technologies,
c1990

Rice Rocket
by Alex Shoeb
for Lib Technologies,
1997

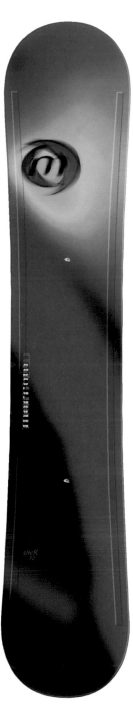

Slick 41
by Jeff Bartel
for Morrow,
1997/98

Slick 46
by Jeff Bartel
for Morrow,
1997/98

Slick 52
by Jeff Bartel
for Morrow,
1997/98

Revert 60
by Jeff Bartel and Mike Byrne
for Morrow,
1997/98

Another one of Todd McFarlane's reigning Spawn women, this super power girl Tiffany snowboard is a free-riding dream, this directional board (longer nose than tail) keeps your forward momentum zooming . Prepare to ride like a Goddess on a mission out of heaven with this board.

tiffany
148 cm

camber depth
edge contact 118 cm
tip width 27.86 cm
tail width 27.86 cm
waist 23.56 cm
sidecut radius 850 cm

angela
151 cm

camber depth
edge contact 118.46 cm
tip width 28.1 cm
tail width 28.1 cm
waist 24.00 cm
sidecut radius 790 cm

Goddess Snowboards merged with Todd McFarlane of Image Comics to bring you, Angela. 151 cm makes this directional (longer nose than tail) board cut through, powder like a hot spoon through ice cream! Watch out for envious comic collecting boys trying to snake this board from you—although this board is strong enough for a man it's made for a woman!

54

51

48

45

154 surf safari　　　　151 angela　　　　148 tiffany　　　　145 sidewalk surfer　　　　141 betsey johnson　　　　136 cookie

g

animal art. kristin kohrs.

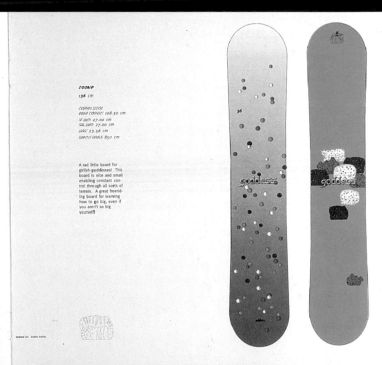

cookie
136 cm

GODDESS SHAPE
EFFECTIVE EDGE / CONTACT 108.50 cm
TIP WIDTH 27.00 cm
TAIL WIDTH 27.00 cm
WAIST 23.56 cm
SIDECUT RADIUS 8.50 cm

A rad little board for girlish-goddesses! This board is nice and small enabling constant control through all sorts of terrain. A great freeriding board for learning how to go big, even if you aren't so big yourself!

36

Previous two pages.
Goddess catalogue,
1997 designed by
Scott Clum.
Board graphics
designed by
Susie Larson.

Revert 54
by Jeff Bartel and Mike Byrne
for Morrow,
1997/98

Revert 51
by Jeff Bartel and Mike Byrne
for Morrow,
1997/98

Revert 47
by Jeff Bartel and Mike Byrne
for Morrow,
1997/98

Revert 43
by Jeff Bartel and Mike Byrne
for Morrow,
1997/98

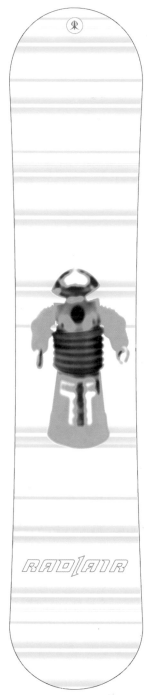

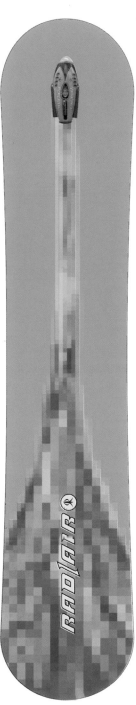

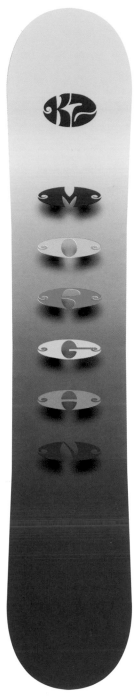

Indis 110, base
by Marcel Langenegger
for Rad/Air, 1997/98

Indis 153, base
by Marcel Langenegger
for Rad/Air, 1997/98

Indis 120, base
by Marcel Langenegger
for Rad/Air, 1997/98

Morgan pro model, base
by Michael Strassburger,
Modern Dog for K2, 1996

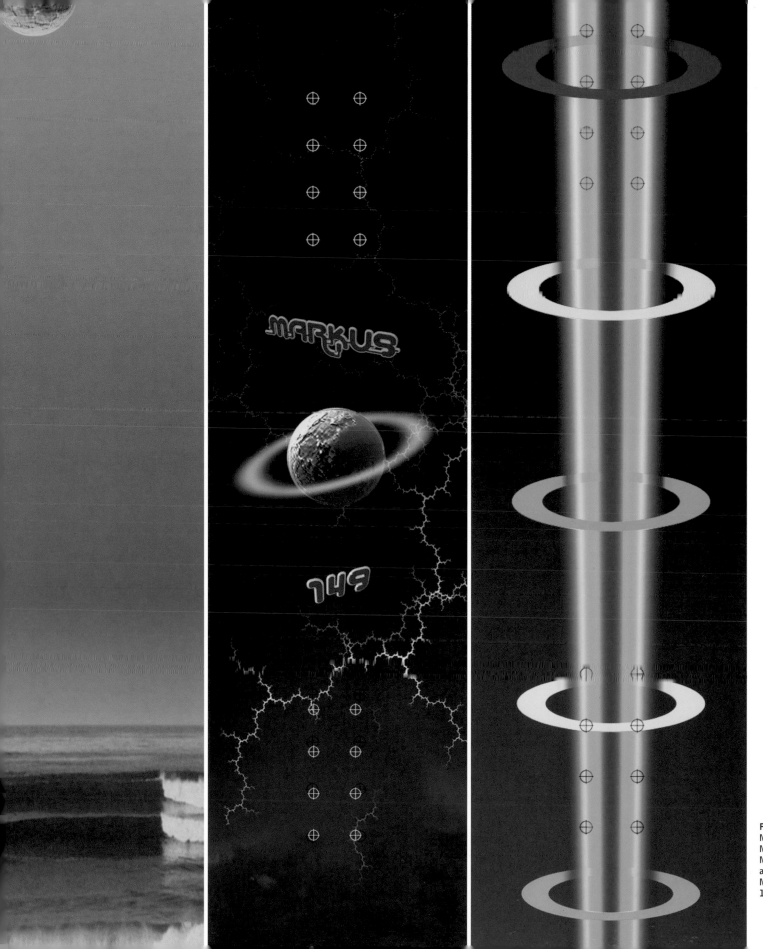

MARKUS

149

From left:
Markus pro model, base;
Markus pro model, top;
Morgan pro model, top;
all by Michael Strassburger,
Modern Dog for K2,
1996

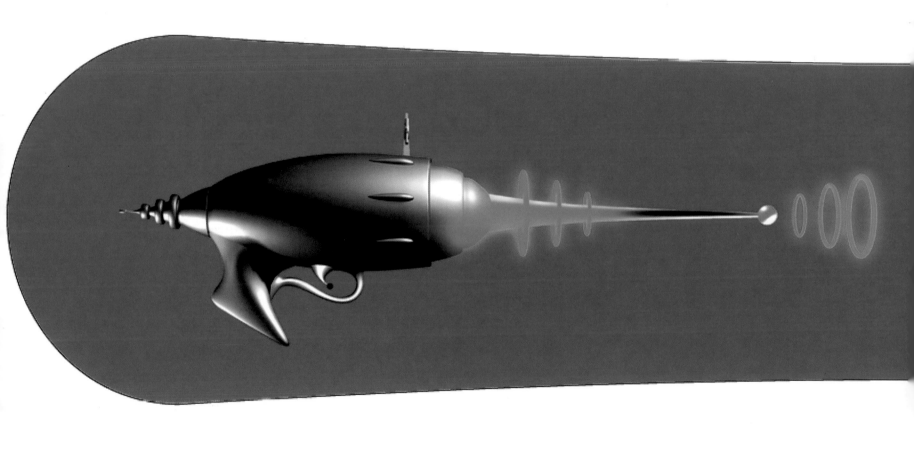

Indis 159, base
by Marcel Langenegger
for Rad/Air,
1997/98

"OUR BALSA WOOD IS HAND SELECTED
BY MEN ON HORSES WEARING WHITE
HATS IN ECUADOR. IF THE WOOD FROM A
VILLAGE IS NO GOOD, EVERYONE DIES."

From Lib Technologies 1997 catalogue

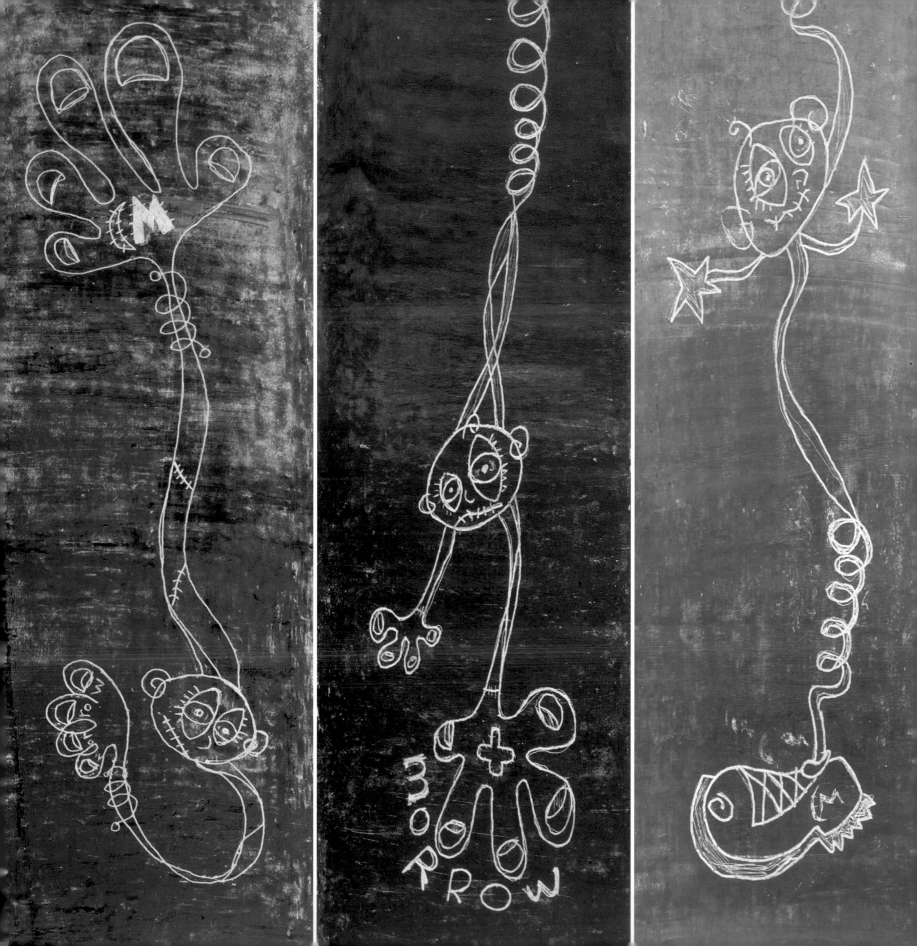

Escape 47, top
by Jeff Bartel for
Morrow, 1997/98

Escape 53, top
by Jeff Bartel for
Morrow, 1997/98

Escape 59, top
by Jeff Bartel for
Morrow, 1997/98

Escape 64, top
by Jeff Bartel for
Morrow, 1997/98

Left to right:
Escape 47, base
Escape 53, base
Escape 59, base
By Lyle Motley
for Morrow,
1997/98

Master 63
by Jeff Bartel and
Mike Byrne for
Morrow, 1997/98

Master 57
by Jeff Bartel and
Mike Byrne for
Morrow, 1997/98

Master 69
by Jeff Bartel and
Mike Byrne for
Morrow, 1997/98

Master 52
by Jeff Bartel and
Mike Byrne for
Morrow, 1997/98

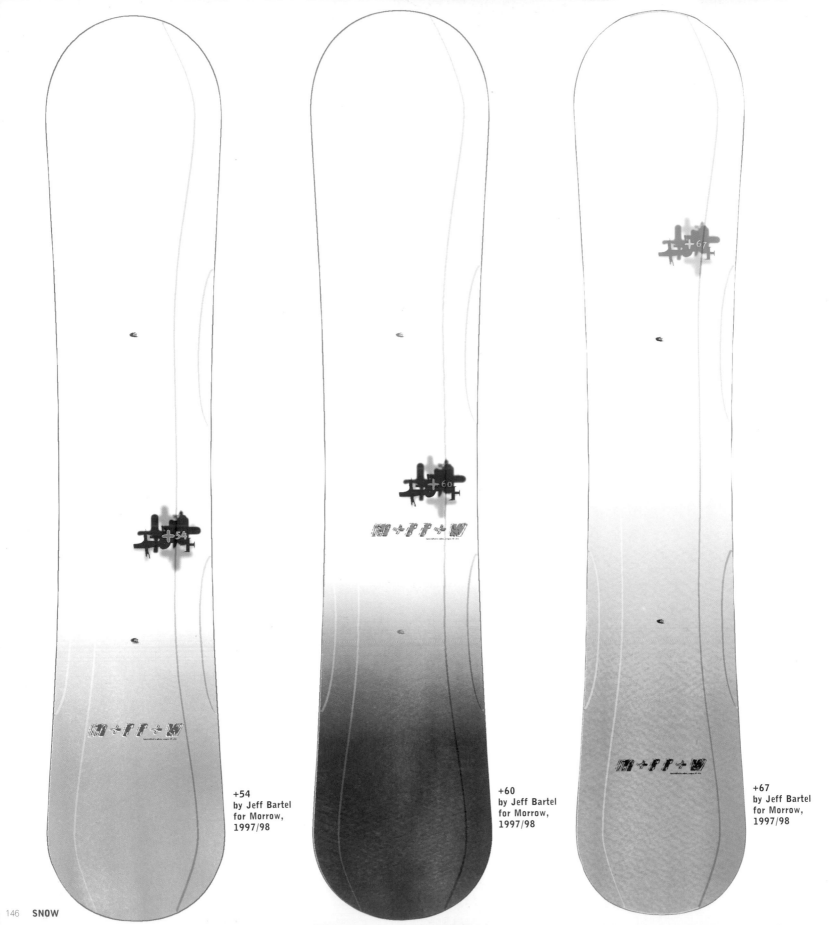

+54
by Jeff Bartel
for Morrow,
1997/98

+60
by Jeff Bartel
for Morrow,
1997/98

+67
by Jeff Bartel
for Morrow,
1997/98

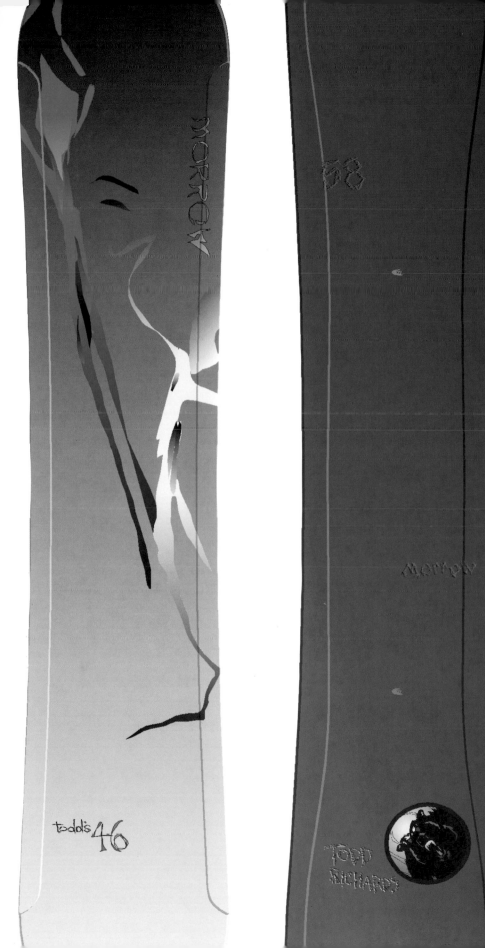

Left to right:
tr46, tr58, tr54
Todd Richards
pro boards
Original drawings
by Todd Richards,
art directed by
Morrow design
team, 1997/98

The Attik Design,
1997
Proposals for
snowboard graphics

The Attik Design, 1997
Proposals for snowboard graphics

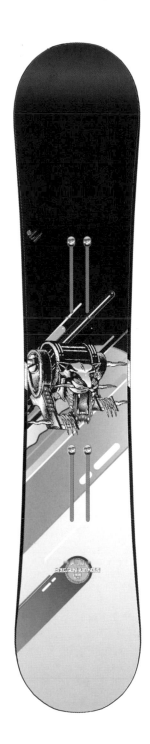

Bjorn Leines series,
art director Jared Eberhardt,
designer/illustrator Paul Brown for Forum 2002
The pro wanted to incorporate five styles of martial arts into the graphics, represented by the different animals featured

Proline series,
designed by Desdoigts & Associés (Paris) for Rossignol,
creative director Olivier Desdoigts, design team Arnaud Perrier,
Alberic Goudard and Stephane Sardet, 2002

Premier series,
designed by Desdoigts & Associés
(Paris) for Rossignol,
creative director Olivier Desdoigts,
design team Arnaud Perrier, Alberic
Goudard and Stephane Sardet, 2002

Canyon 67,
design director Lance Violette,
designers Michael Jager,
Shintaro Tanabe, Lance Violette
at JDK for Burton, 2002

Republik 63,
design director Lance Violette,
designer Denis Kegler at JDK,
illustrator Scott Leonhardt for
Burton, 2002

Dominant 56,
design director Lance Violette
at JDK, designer/illustrator
Noah Butkus for Burton, 2002

Feelgood 148,
design director Lance Violette,
designer Craig Melchiand at JDK,
illustrator Sabrina Ward Harrison
for Burton, 2002

Dragon 58,
design director Lance Violette,
designer/illustrator Jason Selke
at JDK for Burton, 2002
Creative director for all Burton
boards shown: Michael Jager

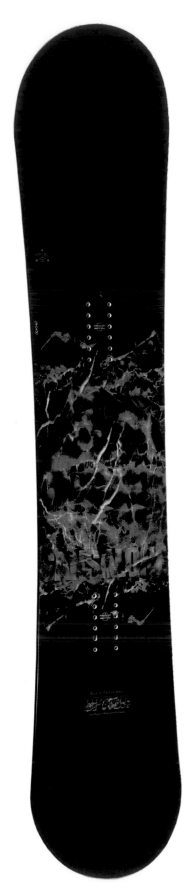

Left to right: Sancalone,
Signature, Vinson and Free Plus,
all by John Culvin for Option, 2001

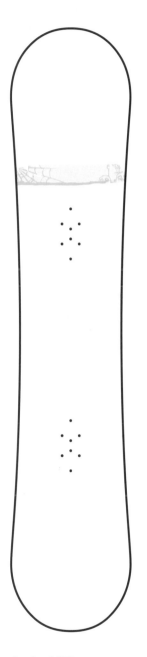

Punch 34,
design director Lance Violette,
designer Cody Hudson at JDK,
illustrator Me Company
for Burton, 2001
Creative director for all Burton
boards shown: Michael Jager

Rush 60,
design director Lance Violette
at JDK, designer Andy Jenkins,
illustrator Geoff McFetridge
for Burton, 2001

Rush 60,
design director Lance Violette,
designer Malcolm Buick at JDK,
illustrator Dave Kinsey
for Burton, 2002

Dominant 152,
design director Lance Violette
at JDK, designer/illustrator Noah
Butkus for Burton, 2002
The board came with a pack of
stencils (left) to make your own
graphics

FROM
EXTREME
TO
MAINSTREAM

The original edition of this book was an exercise in bringing a distinct, vibrant visual culture to the attention of the wider world. We wanted to illustrate that graphic design played an integral part in surfing, skateboarding and snowboarding, albeit to a varying degree. Through graphics, these sports communicated their culture and ideals. Particularly in skateboarding, where the boards themselves are practically identical, graphics became virtually the only means of distinguishing one manufacturer's product from another. Here was an activity that had become a way of life and it expressed its unique culture via graphic design.

Were we to embark on such a project today, however, there would be no such sense of exploring uncharted territory. In the intervening years, board culture, or more accurately, skateboard culture, has become mainstream. Its attitude and visual language have been co-opted, hijacked perhaps, by the art and media world at large, drawn by its spirit and energy. Its anti-corporate, no bullshit agenda is hugely attractive to No Logo-reading, anti-WTO-protesting youth. As is its addiction to stupid stunts: MTV's Jackass show and its host of imitators are drawn directly from skate culture and the videos put out by manufacturers. Its production team and presenters are mostly either skaters or are involved somehow in the skateboard industry. And the Extreme Sports phenomenon also shares much of board sports' audience and attitude.

Board culture is also expressed through one of the biggest recent music scenes – nu-metal. Bands and their fans borrow extensively from board culture, not just in clothing but in attitude. In film, renegade director Larry Clark has made skaters and their lives the central theme of his work, becoming an evangelist of the lifestyle and even taking up the sport, aged 47. "There is more life in a skateboarder skating down the street than in a hundred Hollywood actors," he has been quoted as saying.

Fashion, of course, has shown an interest. Baggy combat pants and hoodies have made catwalk appearances, while at street level, labels such as Silas, A Bathing Ape and Carhartt are heavily influenced by the culture (Carhartt invited a selection of artists and designers to decorate skateboards for an exhibition which toured its European stores). Burberry even produced a skateboard, complete with trademark checked graphics, for its Autumn/Winter 2001 range of accessories – once it was the makers of The Simpsons employing the skateboard as a symbol of youthful rebellion, now a high fashion house sees it as the perfect complement to its handbags and shoes.

And while at the time of researching the first book, there was already a growing market for boards as art objects, especially surf and skateboards, interest from the visual arts scene in board culture has progressed significantly. Often positioned alongside graffiti artists, board graphics designers are now celebrated in "street art" exhibitions around the world, while the board has become a popular canvas for artists from all genres. There has been a two-way development here: on the one hand, board artists such as Geoff McFetridge have begun to move into the mainstream with commercial illustration commissions (McFetridge has even signed up with a production company to direct music videos). On the other hand, established illustrators such as James Jarvis and Pete Fowler have moved in the other direction with manufacturers such as Heroin and Hessenmob bringing out Illustrator series of boards bearing their designs.

The result of this legitimization of board graphics has been a somewhat heightened sophistication in the output of the skate and snowboard industries from which we have drawn the new content for this edition. When researching the first book, we were made aware of concerns among the skate community, particularly that a growth in the numbers of young boys buying boards was leading to a dumbing down of the graphics with cartoon characters and crude gags becoming the norm. Growth in the industry in the intervening years appears to have forestalled such a visually threatening development, however. It now appears that the skateboard and snowboard industries are big enough to accommodate all tastes. Who would have thought, for example, that there would now be a range of boards sporting illustrations of classic twentieth-century furniture as with Tony Larson's Modern Chair series for Girl? Technological developments have also helped. Instead of the traditional screenprinting, many skateboard companies are now using a new heat transfer process whereby images are output direct from computer to plate. This allows for the unlimited use of colour as well as, for the first time, photographic imagery.

Revisiting the area after a gap of five years, we were delighted to find that the vibrancy and attitude of board graphics remain undimmed, while the added sophistication in approach and technique of the latest work reflects the sports' newly enhanced cultural significance.

THE AUTHORS

Patrick Burgoyne is the editor of leading communication arts magazine, Creative Review, and the author of several design books
Jeremy Leslie is Creative Director at John Brown Citrus Publishing, London and is author of the highly successful book Issues: New Magazine Design

ACKNOWLEDGEMENTS

Additional research Sharon Lake
Divider page photographs by Geoff Kula (intro), Jeremy Leslie (surf), Rick Kosick (skate) and Stevan Keane (snow)
Action photographs Page 17 by Warren Bolster for Local Motion, page 50 Stereo pro Greg Hunt, supplied by Deluxe, page 111 supplied by Rad Air
Additional photography by Richard Dean
Special thanks to the following Jim Phillips, Johnny Rice, Matt Micuda, Bill Stewart, Mitch McEwen, Marcio Zouvi, Jamie Buckingham, everyone at Mambo, Moish Brenman, Steve Ruge, Todd Francis, Andy Jenkins, Misha Hollenbach, Erik Brunetti, Jim Knight, Mike Lesage, John Thomas, Marc McKee, Rick Kosick, Micki Vuckovich, Brian Krezel, Jason Irwin, John Hersey, J. Otto Seibold, Shep Fairey, Scott Clum, Sean Donnell, all at JDK (especially Lance Violette), Robynne Raye, Paul Gruber, Stephan Lauhoff, Steve Wills, Jeff Bartel, Mike Dawson, Carlos Segura, Mark Foster, Jared Eberhardt, Tony Larson and everyone who helped in the making of this book

BORED